Introducing Jesus Christ

Emeka Nwankpa

New Wine Press

New Wine Press
PO Box 17
Chichester
West Sussex PO20 6YB
England

Unless otherwise stated, all Bible quotations are from the KJV, King James Version.

NKJV – New King James Version. © Copyright 1983 Thomas Nelson Inc, Box 141000, Nashville, TN 37214 USA.

NASB – The New American Standard Bible. © Copyright The Lockman Foundation, 1960, 1962, 1963, 1968, 1971, 1972, 1973, 1975, 1977. La Habra, California.

ISBN: 1 874367 30 2

Typeset by CRB (Drayton) Typesetting Services, Norwich
Printed in England by Clays Ltd, St Ives plc.

Contents

Foreword

Emeka Nwankpa, a lawyer by profession, is well known in Nigeria for the prophetic ministry which he exercises. His energy and zeal for the Lord Jesus are carried over into all his activities, and are particularly to be seen in his tireless seizing of every opportunity to witness to his faith.

That faith and commitment to Christ is clearly communicated throughout the pages of this book. The author's great desire is expressed in the title; it is 'Introducing Jesus Christ' to all who will listen.

This book is written with a simplicity and clarity of style that will be helpful both to the new believer and to the seeker. It will also be a faith-builder for those who have been believers for a long time and who are looking for a book about Jesus which highlights his relationships with people, his love and compassion for the poor, the sick and the needy.

The book does not attempt to be an exegetical or historical survey of the Gospel accounts of the life of Jesus. Rather, it looks at a selection of incidents in the ministry of Jesus which illustrate the way in which Jesus dealt with some of the people whom he encountered.

The final chapters of the book deal with the atoning death of Jesus upon the Cross and his glorious resurrection. The focus here is on the central truths of our faith, the transforming power of the Cross for the lives of those who come in repentance and humility to Jesus.

I have no doubt that this book will bring a blessing to many in helping to introduce them to Jesus, the Name above all names, the only Name through which we are saved, and who is the only way to the Father.

Clifford Hill
PWM Team Ministries
London, England

February 1994

Introduction

It may seem ironic that one should write a book introducing Jesus Christ when his return is in fact so imminent.

Yet I believe firmly that this is an enterprise which is inspired by the Holy Spirit to enable people to really know Jesus Christ in these tumultuous times.

So much has happened, so much is happening and yet so much more will soon happen. In the midst of all these shakings, chaos and judgements it is important for men to see the facts about Jesus and embrace him as Saviour, Messiah and King because he is the Prince of Peace.

In these times, if one knows and holds firm to Jesus, life would be meaningful. The frustrations of life would be less traumatic and when the time comes the Lord will take such a one to heaven for the next phase in God's plan...

Chapter 1

The Promised One

Jesus Christ is the only begotten Son of God sent into the world as a gesture of God's love towards mankind so that men would not perish but be saved.

> 'For God so loved the world, that he gave his only begotten Son, that whosoever believeth in him should not perish, but have everlasting life.' (John 3:16)

His coming into the world became necessary because of the fall of man through sin and rebellion against God's Command. The incident of man's fall is recorded in Genesis 3. In speaking to the serpent God promised to send the seed of the woman:

> 'And I will put enmity between thee and the woman, and between thy seed and her seed; it shall bruise thy head, and thou shalt bruise his heel.' (Genesis 3:15)

God redeemed this promise in sending Jesus Christ when the time fell due. The record of the fulfilment is found in Galatians 4:4–5.

> 'But when the fulness of the time was come, God sent forth his Son, made of a woman, made under the law, To redeem them that were under the law, that we might receive the adoption of sons.'

Jesus came into the world by the miracle of the virgin birth. This was extraordinary. Only God could make such a thing happen. When we remember that God created man and gave man the ability to reproduce, it should not therefore seem to us impossible that the same God could by his Holy Spirit enable a virgin to conceive and bring forth his only begotten son into the world as he had already promised.

> *'Therefore the* LORD *himself shall give you a sign; Behold, a virgin shall conceive, and bear a son, and shall call his name Immanuel.'* (Isaiah 7:14)

This was fulfilled at the appointed time when God sent his angel to go and speak to Mary, a virgin betrothed to Joseph.

> *'And in the sixth month the angel Gabriel was sent from God unto a city of Galilee, named Nazareth,*
> *To a virgin espoused to a man whose name was Joseph, of the house of David; and the virgin's name was Mary.*
> *And the angel said unto her, Fear not, Mary: for thou hast found favour with God.*
> *And, behold, thou shall conceive in thy womb, and bring forth a Son, and shalt call his name* JESUS.
> *He shall be great, and shall be called the Son of the Highest: and the Lord God shall give unto him the throne of his father David;'* (Luke 1:26–27; 30–32)

Naturally the virgin sought clarification from the angel.

> *'Then said Mary unto the angel, How shall this be, seeing I know not a man?*
> *And the angel answered and said unto her, the Holy Ghost shall come upon thee, and the power of the Highest shall overshadow thee: therefore also that holy*

thing which shall be born of thee shall be called the Son of God.'   (Luke 1:34–35)

Jesus was born in a manger in Bethlehem. Angels appeared to the shepherds in the surrounding country side and announced his birth to them.

> *'And there were in the same country shepherds abiding in the field, keeping watch over their flock by night.*
> *And, lo, the angel of the Lord came upon them, and the glory of the Lord shone round about them: and they were sore afraid.*
> *And the angel said unto him, Fear not: for, behold, I bring you good tidings of great joy, which shall be to all people.*
> *For unto you is born this day in the city of David a Saviour, which is Christ the Lord.'*   (Luke 2: 8–11)

God had brought the Saviour into the world. Jesus was born as a human being for a very important reason. He would eventually have to die for the sins of mankind and he therefore took upon himself the seed of Abraham.

> *'Forasmuch then as the children are partakers of flesh and blood, he also himself likewise took part of the same; that through death he might destroy him that had the power of death, that is, the devil;'*
> (Hebrews 2:14)

Jesus became the son of man. He was made a little lower than the angels for the suffering of death. It is important to stress this fact that Jesus came as a man. It is one of the cardinal truths of the Christian faith. The significance of this is very deep. He identified with man in every way except that he never committed sin. It was God's deliberate plan that Jesus should come into the world as a man.

> *'But we see Jesus, who was made a little lower than the angels for the suffering of death, crowned with glory and honour; that he by the grace of God should taste death for every man.'*   (Hebrews 2:9)

One very obvious fact here is that Jesus humbled himself to become a man because of God's love for mankind. This also shows his humility. We are commanded therefore as believers to have the mind of Christ.

> *'Let this mind be in you, which was also in Christ Jesus:*
>
> *Who, being in the form of God, thought it not robbery to be equal with God:*
>
> *But made himself of no reputation, and took upon him the form of a servant, and was made in the likeness of men:*
>
> *And being found in fashion as a man, he humbled himself, and became obedient unto death, even the death of the cross.'*   (Philippians 2:5–8)

When we read that Jesus took upon him the form of a man, it is clear that he did it out of a deliberate choice for the purpose of our salvation and redemption. He did so because he was embarking on a rescue mission to seek and save lost mankind. His being born as a man opened him up to Satan's attacks and to temptations. Yet he faced all of it and overcame without failing or falling or faltering even once. This fact should set Jesus apart in a class by himself in our contemplation and should also inspire confidence in him, who he is and what he came to accomplish for us.

> *'Seeing then that we have a great high priest, that is passed unto the heavens, Jesus the Son of God, let us hold fast our profession. For we have not an high priest which cannot be touched with the feeling of our infirmities; but was in all points tempted like as we are, yet without sin.*

*Let us therefore come boldly unto the throne of grace,
that we may obtain mercy, and find grace to help in
time of need.'* (Hebrews 4:14–16)

Jesus Christ was perfect, sinless and holy. Nobody
could accuse him of any sin. In the course of his ministry
he asked the Jews.

*'Which of you convinceth me of sin?
And if I say the truth, why do ye not believe me?'*
(John 8:46)

None of his disciples could point to any sin he committed. In fact if he had done any wrong at least Judas
Iscariot could have blown the whistle on him. It is significant that after he betrayed his master, Judas cried *'I have
betrayed innocent blood'* (Matthew 27:4). Peter in his own
testimony later has this to say:

*'For even hereunto were ye called: because Christ also
suffered for us, leaving us an example, that ye should
follow his steps:
Who did no sin, neither was guile found in his mouth:
Who, when he was reviled, reviled not again; when he
suffered, he threatened not; but committed himself to
him that judgeth righteously:
Who his own self bare our sins in his own body on the
tree, that we, being dead to sins, should live unto
righteousness: by whose stripes ye were healed.'*
(1 Peter 2:21–24)

Even the Roman Gentile Judge Pilate who tried him
found no fault in him.

*'And Pilate, when he had called together the chief
priests and the rulers and the people,
Said unto them, Ye have brought this man unto me, as
one that perverteth the people: and, behold, I, having*

examined him before you, have found no fault in this man touching those things whereof ye accuse him:'
(Luke 23:13, 14)

The evidence so far overwhelmingly proves that Jesus Christ was a sent one and a unique man from God to take on the assignment of man's salvation.

Chapter 2

Two Men Who Met Jesus

Any story of any person who meets Jesus is usually a heart moving one. Whether such a person is poor or rich, Jesus deals with people along the lines of certain principles as we shall see in the stories of these two men who met Jesus the same day.

Blind Bartimaeus

'Then it happened, that as He was coming near Jericho, that a certain blind man sat by the road begging.

And hearing a multitude passing by, he asked what it meant.

So they told him that Jesus of Nazareth was passing by.

And he cried out, saying, "Jesus, Son of David, have mercy on me!"

Then those who went before warned him that he should be quiet; but he cried out all the more, "Son of David, have mercy on me!"

So Jesus stood still and commanded him to be brought to Him.

And when he had come near, He asked him, saying "What do you want Me to do for you?" And he said, "Lord, that I may receive my sight."

> *Then Jesus said unto him, "Receive your sight; your faith has saved you."*
> *And immediately he received his sight, and followed Him, glorifying God.*
> *And all the people, when they saw it, gave praise to God;'* (Luke 18:35–43 NKJV)

This encounter has many aspects which could encourage anybody and also shows some principles in receiving blessings from Jesus Christ. The man was blind, a beggar relying on the kindness of others. Furthermore he was in a situation where nobody spoke up for him. Lastly he was not saved.

But apparently he had heard about Jesus. He must have been told that Jesus is the Son of David (Matthew 1:1) and that he came from God and had the power to perform miracles.

When his enquiry as to what was happening around yielded the answer that Jesus was passing that way he made up his mind to receive his healing.

We must take note that he had faith in the identity and person of Jesus as the Messiah.

He also believed that Jesus had the power to exercise mercy on him to bring healing. He took a step of boldness and began calling out *'Jesus, thou Son of David, have mercy on me.'*

Immediately he ran into unquantifiable opposition. People who were part of the crowd and who felt he was being a nuisance told him to shut up. But he shouted even louder to be heard over the noise of the crowd. He was dead to public opinion and was determined to seize that moment. Whatever anybody felt or thought about him did not at all worry him.

He shouted so loud that Jesus stopped. Jesus stood still. Think of it. Jesus, the Son of God, the one for whom and by whom all things were made stood still. Jesus temporarily forgot the crowd. He forgot the next appointment and stood still for a beggar sitting in the dust by the road side. He then commanded that Bartimaeus – for this was the blind man's name, be brought. Immediately public opinion changed. Those who had a short time earlier told him to keep quiet now said *'Be of good cheer, the Master is calling you.'* Bartimaeus jumped up, tore off his rags and went forward towards the voice of the Master.

At this point the crowd stood still. The kingdom of darkness would have become nervous because one victim would soon be lost.

Jesus then asked a question – *'What do you want me to do for you?'* Bartimaeus could possibly have asked for anything since it was an open-ended question. This was to teach the crowd and us a lesson. In dealing with Jesus we have got to be specific. The cry *'Have mercy on me!'* can draw his attention, but to meet our needs he must have a specific request from us.

Bartimaeus was prompt and clear in his request – *'That I may receive my sight.'* Jesus then spoke.

'Receive your sight; your faith has saved you.'
(Luke 18:42 NKJV)

Bartimaeus received his sight, came out of that world of darkness and perpetual night to be able to see. In addition he got **saved**. His faith and his recognition of who Jesus was pulled him through. We can know Jesus by faith.

This encounter brings out a few facts about Jesus. He responds to faith. He ministers to those who come to him. He gives individual attention and he is not a respecter of persons.

Bartimaeus thereupon jumped from the dust of the roadside to Jericho into the pages of God's word – the Bible. Today we learn from his faith. The crowd still remains faceless, a crowd. We do not know their names but this one man's faith has made him an everlasting example of what Jesus can do.

17

Zacchaeus

> *'Then Jesus entered and passed through Jericho.*
> *Now behold, there was a man named Zacchaeus who*
> *was a chief tax collector, and he was rich.*
> *And he sought to see who Jesus was, but could not*
> *because of the crowd, for he was of short stature.*
> *So he ran ahead and climbed up into a sycamore tree*
> *to see Him, for He was going to pass that way.*
> *And when Jesus came to the place, He looked up and*
> *saw him, and said to him, "Zacchaeus, make haste*
> *and come down, for today I must stay at your house."*
> *So he made haste and came down, and received Him*
> *joyfully. But when they saw it, they all murmured,*
> *saying, "He has gone to be a guest with a man who is a*
> *sinner."*
> *Then Zacchaeus stood and said to the Lord, "look,*
> *Lord, I give half of my goods to the poor; and if I have*
> *taken anything from anybody by false accusation, I*
> *restore fourfold."*
> *And Jesus said to him, "Today salvation has come to*
> *this house, because he also is a son of Abraham;*
> *"for the Son of Man has come to seek and to save that*
> *which was lost."'*   (Luke 19:1–10 NKJV)

This second encounter with Jesus followed the same day after the one in our last story.

Zacchaeus, this rich chief tax collector, must have heard so much about Jesus. He must have been told of his teachings, power and wisdom. It is important to point out a few things about Zacchaeus. To have risen to a chief tax-collector in the Roman colonial government he must have known the ropes – how to grease palms here and there, and if it were today he could have belonged to one or two cults.

He would have naturally made most guest lists because people would want to curry favour from him and be in his good books.

But despite all of these things there was a vacuum in the

life of Zacchaeus. An emptiness was there in his heart that his wealth and position could not fill. He came out of his well appointed office when news got to him that Jesus was in Jericho because he wanted to see him. It is clear from the text that the two had never met. As Zacchaeus approached two things conspired to threaten his ambition to see Jesus. The first was the crowd. There were so many people and furthermore with the opening of the eyes of Bartimaeus the excitement must have been very strong in that crowd. Secondly he was a short man.

Thinking quickly he must have discarded the thought of quietly going home. In his desperation to see this man he, a rich well known name, clambered up a sycamore tree.

It was an act of faith for a rich man to do this. The newspapers could easily today have carried photographs and captions reporting this kind of faux pas. Again this act showed that Zacchaeus was prepared to die to public opinion.

Unknown to Zacchaeus the Lord Jesus Christ knew the desire he had and knew his name by a word of knowledge.

When Jesus drew level with that tree he looked up and called Zacchaeus by his name and added that he, Jesus, would be going to his home!

What a surprise. Zacchaeus quickly came down and joyfully received him. At this point the crowd murmured that Jesus had gone to be a guest to a man who was a sinner. It is ironic that other sinners were of the opinion that Zacchaeus was a sinner! He must have been really notorious.

His reputation amounted to nothing.

And yet that draws us to see another fact about Jesus. He is not ashamed or afraid of our reputation when we desire him.

Again for the second time in one day Jesus forgot the crowd and ministered to one soul who really wanted him and thirsted after him. He is not a respecter of persons. This time he ministered to a rich man.

When they got to Zacchaeus' house the man confessed

his guilt and indicated his willingness to turn over a new leaf and make restitution.

Jesus brought salvation unto the home of Zacchaeus that day.

An encounter with Jesus can bring salvation, healing, joy, a miracle and deliverance. He came to seek and to save that which was lost.

You too can have an encounter with him.

Chapter 3

Two Women Who Encountered Jesus

Jesus not only ministered to men but also to women. Each story highlights the patience and compassion of Jesus in dealing with people and bringing them to salvation. The encounters of the two women under discussion in this chapter point out that even when we do not understand or are misunderstood, He, **Jesus**, understands our deepest problems and is ever ready to help us out.

The Woman at the Well of Samaria

This story is found in the fourth chapter of the Gospel of John in the Bible. Jesus was on his way to Galilee and passed through Samaria. When he and his disciples got to the city of Sychar, he rested at a well while they went into town to buy food. It was at this time, when he was alone sitting by the well, that the Samaritan woman came to draw water.

Jesus said to her,

> *'Give Me a drink.'*   (John 4:7 NKJV)

The woman must have guessed from his accent that he was a Jew so she retreated behind the wall of racial prejudice. She said to him,

> *'How is it that You, being a Jew, ask a drink from me, a Samaritan woman?'*   (John 4:9 NKJV)

The Bible added in verse 9 that Jews had no dealings with Samaritans. This was a problem that had arisen from the time when Tilgathpileser an Assyrian King sent his general Asnapper to capture and take away all the men from the Northern Kingdom into exile. Not only this, the Assyrians brought in their own men to have children with the women of the Northern Kingdom thus producing a 'mongrel' race called the Samaritans. The pure Jews despised them and the resulting mutual enmity kept them apart. This was what the woman was referring to by her statement.

Then Jesus answered by saying,

> *'If you knew the gift of God, and who it is who says to you, "Give Me a drink," you would have asked Him, and He would have given you living water.'*
>
> (John 4:10 NKJV)

By her answer the woman revealed her second problem, ignorance, when she said,

> *'Sir, You have nothing to draw with, and the well is deep. Where then do You get that living water?'*
>
> (John 4:11 NKJV)

Her ignorance can be understood now because she did not know who was speaking to her and what power he possessed.

She asked Jesus if he was greater than their father Jacob who gave them the well and had drunk from it himself.

To help her further, Jesus said,

> *'Whoever drinks of this water will thirst again, but whoever drinks of the water that I shall give him will never thirst. But the water that I shall give him will become in him a fountain of water springing up into everlasting life.'*   (John 4:13–14 NKJV)

It would appear that at this point the woman could see a glimmer of benefit that could accrue to her from this conversation. She then exposed a third problem by her answer. She was selfish, she wanted the gift but would not receive the person of the Giver.

The woman said to Him

> *'Sir, give me this water, that I may not thirst, nor come here to draw.'* (John 4:15 NKJV)

She was thinking that Jesus was speaking of ordinary natural water. Jesus then said to her,

> *'Go, call your husband, and come here.'* (John 4:16 NKJV)

Matters were now coming to a head and by this statement Jesus, already knowing what would happen, wanted to draw out her remaining problems.

The woman said

> *'I have no husband.'* (John 4:17 NKJV)

Her answer is a classic example of evasion, half a truth and a refusal to make a full disclosure.

Jesus gave her a word of knowledge by revealing the history of her life with men and thereby exposing her fourth problem, sin. She was living with a man who was not her husband.

> *'You have well said, "I have no husband"; for you have had five husbands, and the one whom you now have is not your husband; this you have said truly.'* (John 4:17–18 NASB)

The conversation had truly now been lifted to the spiritual realm. Now realising she was fast running out of evasive options she could only say,

'Sir, I perceive that You are a prophet.'
(John 4:19 NKJV)

But to quickly switch off the searchlight that was now exposing the innermost secrets of her soul, she tried another subterfuge, taking refuge behind the wall of religion. She went on,

'Our fathers worshipped in this mountain, and you people say that in Jerusalem is the place where men ought to worship.' (John 4:20 NASB)

This move exposed her fifth problem. She was taking solace in a dead religion. A religion full of rituals that could not free the worshippers from sin. She had religion but not salvation. Jesus quickly dealt with that problem by telling her how God wanted to be worshipped and who the true worshippers are. Jesus said to her,

'Woman, believe Me, an hour is coming when neither in this mountain, nor in Jerusalem, shall you worship the Father.
You worship that which you do not know; we worship that which we know, for salvation is from the Jews.
But an hour is coming, and now is, when the true worshippers shall worship the Father in spirit and truth; for such people the Father seeks to be His worshippers. God is Spirit, and those who worship Him must worship in spirit and truth.'

(John 4:21–24 NASB)

A lot of people in the world today do not know what they worship. They have not experienced salvation neither do they worship God in spirit and truth. Jesus said of himself,

'I am the way, the truth, and the life: no man cometh unto the Father, but by me.' (John 14:6 KJV)

The woman now made one last move to evade the truth. She retreated to the last option – procrastination. She said,

> '*I know that Messiah is coming (He who is called Christ); when that One comes, He will declare all things to us.*' (John 4:25 NASB)

What in effect she was saying was this – Our conversation has gone too uncomfortably close to the weaknesses of my life. Let us put if off till the future when the Messiah will come; Jesus then dropped the bombshell by saying,

> '*I, who speak to you am He.*' (John 4:26 NASB)

What else was there to say now? This woman was face to face with the Messiah, the One whom she said would explain all things. Her six walls had collapsed and now she was so convicted that she believed in him as the Christ, the Messiah, the sent One.

We see this from her next line of action and her words.

She left her waterpot and went into the city. Natural water was now not the immediate priority. Her encounter with Jesus and its effect in her soul was too much and had to be shared. Her prejudice vanished, her old religion vanished. She accepted all she had done and now proclaimed the Messiah who had come to reconcile her to God.

So she went into the city saying to the men,

> '*Come, see a man who told me all the things that I have done; this is not the Christ, is it?*'
> (John 4:29 NASB)

This announcement and testimony brought many more people coming to the well to meet Jesus. Seeing the effect and excitement upon the woman they invited him into the city.

Tribal and racial prejudices were overtaken. And after a few days the people announced after they believed His word,

> *'It is no longer because of what you said that we believe, for we have heard for ourselves and know that this One is indeed the Savior of the world.'*
>
> (John 4:42 NASB)

The wisdom of the Lord is unbeatable. One woman's repentance and testimony had opened the way for many people to receive and believe in Jesus, the Saviour of the world. Jesus is not a male chauvinist. Women have a place in the Kingdom too.

The Woman Caught in Adultery

This story is recorded in chapter eight of John's gospel. It came out of a conspiracy by the Pharisees to trap Jesus into saying something which would implicate him and thus give them a reason to kill him.

One early morning as Jesus was teaching in the court of the temple the Scribes and the Pharisees brought a woman caught in adultery and set her in the midst of the people. They interrupted his discourse and said to him

> *'Teacher, this woman has been caught in adultery, in the very act.*
> *Now in the Law Moses commanded us to stone such women; what then do You say?'*
>
> (John 8:4–5 NASB)

A number of facts arise for consideration here.

Firstly these hypocrites did not bring the male partner of this woman to face this kangaroo court. Secondly, since they knew what the law of Moses specified, why did they bother Jesus with the question? They should have gone ahead with the execution. Thirdly, if Jesus said, 'do not stone her', he would have been accused of being a fake, not believing in the law of Moses.

Fourthly, if he said, 'stone her', they would have accused him to the Roman colonial authorities as a troublemaker who recommended stoning without their permission. It is to be remembered that when eventually the Jews wanted to crucify Jesus they had to get the approval of the Romans by pressurising Pilate. They thought they had put him in a fix. But they forgot that they were dealing with Jesus, the Son of God.

Jesus knew their plan, their thoughts and above all every detail of their lives including their sins. So instead of arguing, he stooped down and began to write on the sand.

He may have written the names of the first row of people with a list of their sins worthy of death. That would have really convicted and unnerved them when they saw it. They quickly and quietly dropped their stones and moved hastily away.

After writing everyone's name and sins worthy of death the crowd dissolved.

This terribly embarrassed and fearful woman whose reputation had gone and whose nerve had been hanging by a thread was left lying in a heap on the ground waiting for the end to come. Then Jesus said to her,

> *'Woman, where are they? Did no one condemn you?'*
> (John 8:10 NASB)

And she answered,

> *'No one Lord.'*   (John 8:11 NASB)

By that answer, she had recognised him as her Lord. Jesus must have seen the repentance in her heart and then added

> *'Neither do I condemn you; go your way. From now on sin no more.'*   (John 8:11 NASB)

These facts are very clear in this encounter. The Scribes and Pharisees came with pride and malice to Jesus and when their sin and hypocrisy were exposed they failed to take the opportunity to repent.

Secondly Jesus knows the details of everyone's life since he is privy to God's records. Nothing is hid from him about our lives. Finally, a person who is condemned by everybody but repents will be justified by Christ.

The gentle treatment of this repentant woman shows the compassion of Jesus.

- If any, some or all of those Pharisees had acknowledged and confessed their sin like Zacchaeus, Jesus would have forgiven them and they would have experienced salvation. But they went away with their sins.

Chapter 4

Jesus and the Sons of Zebedee

Among the twelve apostles of Jesus were two brothers of the same parents, James and John the sons of Zebedee.

They both helped their father in the fishing business and were partners to Simon Peter in the trade.

When Jesus was recruiting his disciples he walked by the sea of Galilee on one occasion and saw these two men with their father in the boat mending their nets and called them. They followed him.

> *'And walking by the Sea of Galilee, He saw two brothers, Simon who was called Peter, and Andrew his brother, casting a net into the sea; for they were fishermen. And He said to them, "Follow Me, and I will make you fishers of men."*
> *And they immediately left the nets, and followed Him. And going on from there He saw two other brothers, James the son of Zebedee and John his brother, in the boat with Zebedee their father, mending their nets; and He called them.*
> *And they immediately left the boat and their father, and followed Him.'* (Matthew 4:18–22 NASB)

These two men had a peculiar temperament which earned them the nickname *'sons of thunder'* (Mark 3:17). They had a fiery disposition. This can easily be seen in Luke 9:54 when both men wanted the permission of Jesus to command fire to come down upon the Samaritans who refused Jesus passage through their village. They certainly had a quick temper. The odyssey of these two brothers is interesting and instructive. They both willingly followed the Lord leaving their occupation and their father. They soon became very enthusiastic and diligent disciples of Jesus.

Early on in their initial encounter with Jesus, they had seen him borrow Peter's boat. After using it to preach to the crowd leaving the shore Jesus told Peter to cast out further into the sea. Peter protested that they had laboured all night and caught nothing when he was asked to throw the net to the right side. Nevertheless, he said that at the word of the Master he would. And he did. The net caught so much fish in that daytime that he had to call to James and John who came to his rescue to pull the catch in. This was a miracle performed by Jesus in the draught of fishes (Luke 5:1–11).

The effect of this miracle on these two brothers was incalculable. They were so completely overwhelmed that they became totally committed to Jesus.

Having become his disciples they paid particular attention to his teaching and took them to heart deeply. They must have heard Jesus repeatedly teach on the Kingdom and the glory that he would have in it. The prospect of such a wondrous glory enchanted them and they decided to be part of it. They must have discussed it very deeply and seriously and come to a conclusion to present their desire to Jesus. However they may have reasoned that for such a big request, the moral support of their mother would be of great help and that her age could earn them a positive answer from the Lord. So they enlisted her help. She willingly came to be their mouthpiece.

> '*Then the mother of the sons of Zebedee came to Him with her sons, bowing down, and making a request of Him.*

> *And He said to her, "What do you wish?" She said to Him, "Command that in Your kingdom these two sons of mine may sit, one on Your right and one on Your left."*
> *But Jesus answered and said, "You do not know what you are asking for. Are you able to drink the cup that I am about to drink?"*
> *They said to Him, "We are able."*
> *He said to them, "My cup you shall drink; but to sit on My right and on My left, this is not Mine to give, but it is for those for whom it has been prepared by My Father."'* (Matthew 20:20–23 NASB)

Jesus patiently listened to this woman's request on behalf of her children. He did not summarily rebuke them or send them away. He made it clear the positions being asked for were not his to give but belonged to his Father. He told them the truth. But now seeing their desire to obtain more and get places of honour in the kingdom he checked on their commitment by asking two loaded questions.

They did not ask whether the cup or the baptism was of blood or water. They said 'yes we can'. And Jesus took them up on their promise.

These two men thus willingly, as it were, signed up for anything, any suffering that would come their way in order to qualify for a place in the Kingdom of God.

They denied themselves every option that excluded the Kingdom of God.

When the other disciples found out what these two had requested of Jesus they were angry.

> *'And hearing this, the ten became indignant with the two brothers.'* (Matthew 20:24 NASB)

However they did not protest at the price the men had agreed to pay and of course the opinion of the ten did not at all affect the mind of Jesus or his subsequent relationship to these two brothers.

After this conversation we notice that the two brothers entered into the inner circle of Jesus Christ. They were promoted.

Whenever any major miracle was to be performed Jesus took Peter, James and John. This was the case at the healing of the daughter of Jairus.

> *'While He was still speaking, they came from the house of the synagogue official, saying "Your daughter has died; why trouble the Teacher anymore?"*
>
> *But Jesus, overhearing what was being spoken, said to the synagogue official, "Do not be afraid any longer, only believe."*
>
> *And He allowed no one to follow with Him, except Peter and James and John the brother of James.*
>
> *And they came to the house of the synagogue official; and He beheld a commotion, and people loudly weeping and wailing.*
>
> *And taking the child by the hand, He said to her, "Talitha Kum!" (which translated means "Little girl, I say to you, arise").*
>
> *And immediately the girl rose and began to walk; for she was twelve years old. And immediately they were completely astounded.'*
>
> (Mark 5:35–38, 41–42 NASB)

When Jesus went up to the mountain of Transfiguration to meet Moses and Elijah as part of his preparation to go to the cross, he took Peter, James and John along for this memorable event.

> *'And six days later Jesus took with Him Peter and James and John his brother, and brought them up to a high mountain by themselves.*
>
> *And he was transfigured before them; and His face shone like the sun, and His garments became as white as light.'* (Matthew 17:1–2 NASB)

This was a very unique experience which the other nine did not have the privilege of witnessing. They actually saw the transfiguration of Jesus take place and heard the voice of God the Father out of the cloud saying,

> *'This is my beloved Son, with whom I am well-pleased; listen to Him!'* (Matthew 17:5 NASB)

In the Garden of Gethsemane as Jesus awaited the arrival of the mob that would arrest him, he was in agony of soul. Of the remaining eleven disciples, he drew Peter, James and John aside and shared his heart with them requesting them to watch in prayer with him.

> *'And they came to a place named Gethsemane, and He said to His disciples, "Sit here until I have prayed."*
> *And He took with Him Peter and James and John and began to be very distressed and troubled.*
> *And He said to them, My soul is deeply grieved to the point of death; remain here and keep watch.'*

The men shared a little of the burden that Jesus was carrying on his heart as he prepared to go to the Cross to give his life as a sacrifice for the sins of the world. They were called to a higher level of fellowship with Jesus in prayer.

Much later, James was one of the first martyrs.

> *'Now about that time Herod the king laid hands on some who belonged to the church, in order to mistreat them.*
> *And he had James the brother of John put to death with a sword.'* (Acts 12:1–2 NASB)

By this sacrifice he had discharged his commitment to be baptised with the baptism that his master was baptised with and to drink the cup of death. More than that he became beneficiary to the promise which Jesus made:

> *'He that findeth his life shall lose it: and he that loseth
> his life for my sake shall find it.'*   (Matthew 10:39)

John, however, became an old man. He lived long
enough to write the gospel according to St John which is
different from the other three so-called synoptic gospels.
A close study of it would reveal that he wrote with a
deeper spiritual knowledge of Jesus. It was he who
recorded the very important conversation that Jesus had
with Nicodemus, the member of the Sanhedrin who came
to Him by night. This record has facilitated the salvation
of countless souls. It is so helpful.

> *'Now there was a man of the Pharisees, named Nic-
> odemus, a ruler of the Jews; this man came to Him by
> night, and said to Him, "Rabbi, we know that You
> have come from God as a teacher; for no one can do
> these signs that You do unless God is with him."*
> *Jesus answered and said to him,*
> *"Truly, truly, I say to you, unless one is born again,
> he cannot see the Kingdom of God."*
> *Nicodemus said to Him, "How can a man be born
> when he is old? He cannot enter a second time into his
> mother's womb and be born, can he?"*
> *Jesus answered, "Truly, truly, I say to you, unless one
> is born of water and the Spirit, he cannot enter into the
> Kingdom of God.*
> *"That which is born of the flesh is flesh, and that which
> is born of the Spirit is spirit.*
> *"Do not marvel that I said to you, 'You must be born
> again.'"'*   (John 3:1–7 NASB)

Even after that the Lord still singled out John for even
the greatest revelation any human being has ever
received, far beyond that of Moses, the other disciples
and even in some ways higher than that of Paul.

During John's exile in the Isle of Patmos he was in the
Spirit on the Lord's day when he heard a voice speak to
him.

Thus began the series of revelations given to John and which are contained in the last book of the Bible – Revelation.

Every bit of it is charged and powerful. But suffice it to mention here, that John saw Jesus in his glorified state walking in the midst of the seven golden candlesticks, with the seven stars in his right hand. He was clothed in a robe reaching to his feet, and girded across the breast with a golden girdle. His head and his hair were white like white wool, like snow; and his eyes were like a flame of fire. His feet were like burnished bronze, when it has been caused to glow in a furnace, and his voice was like the sound of many waters. Out of his mouth proceeded a sharp sword and his face was like the sun shining at full strength.

No wonder when John saw him in this glorified state he fell down as dead. In the written record of what John saw and heard, we see that God told and showed John things which no other human being had heard or seen.

Jesus reveals many more of his titles and names to John. It is from here that we know that Jesus is the first and the last, the Alpha and the Omega, the One who has the keys of death and of hell.

Furthermore John receives the contents of the seven letters to the Seven Churches in which we still see the problems of the church, the Lord's warnings and the answers to them clearly expressed.

We read of the throne of God, the details of the occasion when Jesus received the Book sealed with seven seals, this book being the Certificate or Deed of Ownership of the Earth from the hand of him that sits on the Throne.

It is John who received the information that Jesus has the key of David and what he shuts no man can open and what he opens no man can shut.

These two brothers have received the glory and reward which are the due of anybody who says 'I will' to Jesus and keeps to this promise.

In concluding this chapter it is necessary to record that

the mother of these two men maintained a vibrant faith in Jesus and was one of the women who were at the crucifixion of Jesus.

> *'And many women who followed Jesus from Galilee, ministering to Him, were there looking on from afar, among whom were Mary Magdalene, Mary the mother of James and Joses, and the mother of Zebedee's sons.'*   (Matthew 27:55–56 NKJV)

Chapter 5

Sitting at the Feet of Jesus

As human beings we live in a world of relationships. Some of these are family, work, societal, professional and other sundry relationships. Each has a certain degree of importance in our lives: But in knowing Jesus it is of the utmost importance to realize that he is our life. It is therefore necessary that we do not allow anything to hinder our relationship with him.

One person who epitomises a good example of how to develop a deep spiritual relationship with Jesus is Mary, the sister of Martha and Lazarus who lived in Bethany.

> *'Now it happened as they went that He entered a certain village; and a certain woman named Martha welcomed Him into her house.*
> *And she had a sister called Mary, who also sat at Jesus' feet and heard His word.*
> *But Martha was distracted with much serving, and she approached Him and said, "Lord, do You not care that my sister has left me to serve alone? Therefore tell her to help me."*
> *And Jesus answered and said to her, "Martha, Martha, you are worried and troubled about many things.*
> *"But one thing is needed, and Mary has chosen that good part, which will not be taken away from her."*
> (Luke 10:38–42 NKJV)

To get the grasp of the import of this story it is appropriate to look deeper into the facts herein.

On the one hand Mary was calm, while Martha was agitated and distracted. Mary wanted to hear the word of the Lord, to know his mind but Martha was busy wanting to serve and to impress the Lord. To enable her hear the word of the Lord, Mary sat at his feet while Martha was in perpetual motion. Mary was not affected by her sister's nerves while Martha went so far as to implicitly accuse Jesus of insensitivity. This is a very heavy thing. It is most serious when we realise that we can work ourselves up into such a state where we take it upon ourselves to advise the Lord or even accuse him of not bothering about things which we brought upon ourselves. Mary's zeal to hear to the Lord pleased him so much while Martha's sullenness drew a rebuke.

Mary was wise because she was getting something that would never be taken from her while Martha was worried about many things. Mary's heart and soul would be refreshed by what the Lord spoke but not so Martha because she did not know the one needful thing. Consider these two sisters of the same parents, resident in the same house being visited by Jesus. Examine their different states of mind which provoked two different reactions from the Lord.

Before we go further it will be instructive to glean a few insights into the kind of mind that Mary had from a few other things she did.

At one time, when Jesus visited the house of Simon the leper in Bethany, while they were eating in that all male luncheon, Mary came into the place and began weeping at the feet of Jesus. She used her tears to wash his feet and her hair to wipe them. Anyone who knows how much women value and take care of their hair would begin to perceive what Mary did here.

She then broke a very costly alabaster box of ointment and proceeded to anoint his feet with it. Jesus explained to the assembly the spiritual significance of what she did.

Mary had come to anoint his body for the burial which was still ahead. And he added that wherever the gospel was preached what she did would be spoken of for a memorial.

Thus her action had come forth from a very devoted heart.

It is this degree of devotion that would enable anyone seek the Lord and sit at his feet to hear from him.

Sitting at the feet of Jesus is a deliberate act of will, we are not asking anything or praying but listening to hear what he would say.

To do this successfully a regular habit of listening to the Lord must be developed. It shows submissiveness. It is at such times that the Lord ministers to our hearts and breaks down the presumptuousness, stubbornness and resistance that are there. It will deliver us from missing God's will, keep us from rebellion and bring constant refreshing when done regularly. Sitting at his feet requires that we empty our minds of all vanity and noise in addition to every distraction.

Jesus was in the constant habit of listening to his Father. In those days when he was here on earth he would go to quiet places and pray. It was one of the secrets of his success. No wonder he could say:

> *'I can of mine own self do nothing:*
> *as I hear, I judge: and my judgment is just;*
> *because I seek not mine own will, but the will of the*
> *Father which hath sent me.'* (John 5:30)

Sitting at his feet is necessary for us to hear from him, to be able to do his will and to do it correctly.

A prayerful study of some of David's psalms shows that he spent time listening to God. He was a prophet and his words show the life of a man who spent time sitting at God's feet and hearing from him. In Psalm 121 he writes:

> *'I will lift up mine eyes unto the hills, from whence*
> *cometh my help. My help cometh from the LORD,*
> *which made heaven and earth.'* (Psalm 121:1–2)

David depended on God. Sitting at his feet is an indication of our inability to help ourselves and it shows our dependence on him. The result of what we hear and receive will make us understand and experience that he will not suffer our feet to be moved, that he is our keeper and that he neither slumbers nor sleeps.

In Psalm 123 David further illustrates the concept of sitting at his feet when he writes:

> *'Unto thee lift I up mine eyes, O thou that dwellest in the heavens. Behold, as the eyes of servants look unto the hand of their masters, and as the eyes of a maiden unto the hand of her mistress; so our eyes wait upon the* Lord *our God, until, that he have mercy upon us.'*
>
> (Psalm 123:1–2)

David would wait upon the Lord until something happened, until God showed mercy upon him in a particular situation.

This ought to be emulated by each believer. This attitude of sitting at his feet, waiting upon him until God does something or says something. It could be on one occasion or it could be a continual thing until we hear from him.

As we sit at his feet, he answers some of the deepest questions we have in our hearts. He removes the stubbornness in our souls, refreshes us from our labours and weariness and opens his heart to us by the Holy Spirit.

As Mary found out, others may have misguided opinions about our agape love for the Lord or even about us as people, but once he appreciates what we do, our hearts will continually receive from him as we sit at his feet.

Spending time in his presence can be extraordinarily rewarding and what we hear at such times could change our lives gloriously.

When we make a habit of sitting at his feet to hear his word we will find that we no longer fret, or get anxious or blown away by winds of worry. Our confidence in him grows and consequently we have holy boldness in the Lord and for the Lord's work.

Chapter 6

Jesus Tests His Disciples

From normal experience we know that in the school systems of the world it is usual for teachers to test their students to see how much they know. This may not be an accurate test of total knowledge but at least it serves as an index that is helpful. In John 6, an occasion arose when Jesus tested his disciples.

> *'After these things Jesus went over the sea of Galilee, which is the sea of Tiberias.*
> *And a great multitude followed him, because they saw his miracles which he did on them that were diseased.*
> *And Jesus went up into a mountain, and there he sat with his disciples.*
> *And the Passover, a feast of the Jews, was nigh.*
> *When Jesus then lifted up his eyes, and saw a great company come unto him, he saith unto Philip.*
> *Whence shall we buy bread, that these may eat?*
> *And this he said to prove (test) him:*
> *for he himself knew what he would do.'* (John 6:1–6)

Here was an emergency of a difficult kind. It was not a joke. About 5,000 men, (women and children not included in that number) had come to Jesus for teaching. After the marathon preaching session it was already becoming dark. Rather than allow the people to go away hungry and run the risk of some fainting on the way, Jesus decided they needed to be fed.

He decided to use this opportunity to test his disciples. He picked on Philip and asked him where they could buy bread so that the people could eat.

It is very important to note that Jesus was not at a loss what to do and neither was he casting around for ideas.

The scripture says clearly, he himself knew what he would do. Whenever we face testings from the Lord it is helpful to know that he already has the answers beforehand.

Philip said two hundred pennyworth of bread would not be enough. He probably was looking at the financial limit of their purse. He said:

> *'Two hundred pennyworth of bread is not sufficient for them, that every one of them may take a little.'*
>
> (John 6:7)

At the very best his vision was that they did not have enough resources for the people to each take a little. One of the disciples Andrew, Simon Peter's brother, reported that a lad had five barley loaves and two small fishes and then asked *'but what are they among so many?'*

These two men were only being human. The financial and material resources at hand would be nothing compared to the mouths that required feeding. And yet Jesus was talking about feeding everybody.

Now having seen and heard the views of his disciples he proceeded to practically demonstrate faith and crisis management for them to see and learn from.

First he said, 'Make the men sit down.' In other words make your troubles, problems sit down. Let there be some order. Do not let the problem control you. Establish control over the situation.

Then he took the loaves and fishes and prayed. They watched him give thanks. Prayer is vital in dealing with problems. Not just a prayer but a prayer of faith with specific requests contained in it.

He then distributed the bread and fishes to his disciples with the command that they should share them out to the seated multitude.

Now for a moment consider yourself in the shoes of one of these disciples. You have a piece of bread which you could easily squeeze into your mouth and it would disappear without a trace but still not satisfy you. And now the Lord says you should proceed to divide it among thousands of people.

It was a very tough situation to be in. But it is made easier if and when we truly understand that it is not our ability but his that does the job at such a moment. This was a high test of faith. Jesus himself had prayed so they proceeded to give out the loaves. I believe that as they broke the bread and gave it out, it multiplied right in their hands.

They kept going until more than five thousand people had been filled. It was not that they each had only a little but that they were all filled despite their various levels of appetite.

In fact the Bible records the aftermath as follows:

> *'When they were filled, he said unto his disciples, Gather up the fragments that remain, that nothing be lost.*
> *Therefore they gathered them together, and filled twelve baskets with the fragments of the five barley loaves, which remained over and above unto them that had eaten.*
> *Then those men, when they had seen the miracle that Jesus did, said, This is of a truth that prophet that should come into the world.'*   (John 6:12–14)

Jesus demonstrated here that he can handle any situation since on our own we would be totally helpless to tackle such problems as would come our way in life and ministry.

He wanted his disciples and us to know that out of tests

can come miracles and glorious experiences once we believe and obey him.

Furthermore he demonstrated that he is able to do exceeding abundantly above all that we ask or think.

Finally the disciples must have realised that Jesus had known what he would do before he even began to ask them. That should boost our faith.

Jesus showed here what I choose to call God's sense of humour. The disciples were twelve in number and the fragments they gathered filled exactly twelve baskets.

Examples of this principle of testing abound in the Bible. And as people who want to walk with God we must understand that we must face it from time to time.

God tested Abraham in Genesis 22. He asked him to bring his son, his only son, whom he loved, and sacrifice Him.

Knowing the number of years Abraham had waited to get this promised son, the trouble he ran into when he consented to take Hagar, who had Ishmael, and the heartache of having to send both of them away, and now to think of sacrificing this son by his own hand!

Nevertheless Abraham obeyed. I believe that he did not discuss this matter with his wife Sarah for obvious reasons. She would have opted to be sacrificed first before he would touch Isaac. Abraham took two servants, travelled for two days before leaving those servants to await his return. He then took Isaac alone for the last part of the journey to mount Moriah and thus took another day.

As they went Isaac innocently asked –

> *'Behold the fire and the wood: but where is the lamb for a burnt offering?'*   (Genesis 22:7)

This must have been a heart wrenching question. Fear, if allowed, could have stopped Abraham.

But from somewhere deep in his spirit he answered:

> *'My son, God will provide himself a lamb for a burnt offering:'*   (Genesis 22:8)

44

When they came to the place which God had told him of Abraham prepared the altar, arranged the wood, laid Isaac and bound him on that altar. Only God knows what was going through the mind of Father and Son at that time.

After this Abraham picked up the knife and raised his hand to strike. At this point an angel of the LORD called him:

> *'Abraham, Abraham...*
> *Lay not thine hand upon the lad,*
> *neither do thou anything unto him:*
> *for now I know that thou fearest God,*
> *seeing thou hast not withheld they son,*
> *thine only son from me.'*   (Genesis 22:11–12)

Abraham proved that he was prepared to obey God and not withhold his son from the Lord.

Following the instruction of the angel he turned and saw a ram caught in a thicket by its horns and he sacrificed it. This ram had been brought from heaven.

That was a type of the lamb slain from the foundation of the world.

As a result of Abraham's obedience God swore by himself to bless him, multiply his seed as the stars of heaven and as the sand on the sea shore and then gave him a promise that his seed shall posses the gates of their enemies (Genesis 22:17).

This test produced for Abraham such eternal blessings. He also saw the ability of God to provide even in the most impossible circumstances. But most importantly God laid the foundation of redemption, using Abraham and Isaac as a shadow of the future sacrifice of Jesus on the cross.

Chapter 7

Jesus Raises Lazarus from the Dead

Jesus was a friend of Lazarus and his sisters Mary and Martha. Occasionally he would visit them if he was passing through Bethany, a village close to Jerusalem.

> *'Now a certain man was sick, named Lazarus, of Bethany, the town of Mary and her sister Martha.*
> *(It was that Mary which anointed the Lord with ointment, and wiped his feet with her hair, whose brother Lazarus was sick.)*
> *Therefore his sisters sent unto him, saying, Lord, behold, he whom thou lovest is sick.'* (John 11:1–3)

Jesus clearly loved Lazarus. His sisters knew this and so when he fell sick they sent a message to Jesus. This was a family where Jesus was much loved. One of them, Mary, had shown two very remarkable qualities. She was prepared to use her very best to honour the Lord and also would sit at his feet to hear his word. When Jesus got this message he said:

> *'This sickness is not unto death, but for the glory of God, that the Son of God might be glorified thereby.'*
> (John 11:4)

Unknown to Lazarus, Mary and Martha, Jesus had decided that this was an opportunity to glorify God and himself. This is a lesson we must learn. The choice was not left with Lazarus or his sisters. In fact they were not consulted. It must be said that Jesus did not say this kind of thing often when he saw the sick.

Jesus definitely loved this family, but decided, because of what he had said earlier, to stay two days where he was. This was not callousness but the determinate counsel of God to glorify himself.

After waiting for the time he thought fit he called his disciples to follow him for the journey to Bethany.

As they travelled, Jesus knew that Lazarus had died and told his disciples so, but his language was different:

> *'Our friend Lazarus sleepeth; but I go, that I may awake him out of sleep.'* (John 11:11)

The disciples did not understand and thought Lazarus was resting in natural sleep. Then Jesus said to them plainly,

> *'Lazarus is dead.*
> *And I am glad for your sakes that I was not there, to the intent ye may believe; nevertheless let us go unto him.'* (John 11:14–15)

Thomas was totally confused and fatalistically faithless. He said that they should all go and die with Lazarus. Some people are like Thomas, unbelieving and hard of hearing when the Lord speaks to them seeking to explain what may be happening around them.

When they finally got to Bethany, Lazarus had been in the grave four days already. Meanwhile mourners, well wishers and friends had been thronging the house of Mary and Martha.

News got to the two sisters that Jesus had finally arrived and was in a certain place. Martha went to see him while Mary stayed back grieving in the house.

On getting there Martha made a very heart rending statement.

> *'Lord, if thou hadst been here, my brother had not died.*
> *But I know, that even now, whatsoever thou wilt ask of God, God will give it thee.'* (John 11:21–22)

Jesus assured her,

> *'Thy brother shall rise again.'* (John 11:23)

Martha mistook this statement as referring **to mean** that Lazarus would rise again in the resurrection at the last day.

At this point Jesus seized the opportunity to introduce himself in a way he had never done before: He usually uses difficult situations to reveal himself more unto his people.

Jesus said unto her,

> *'I am the resurrection,*
> *and the life: he that believeth in me,*
> *though he were dead, yet shall he live:*
> *And whosoever liveth and believeth in me*
> *shall never die. Believest thou this?'*
> (John 11: 25–26)

This was over Martha's head. This new dimension of Jesus' person and power was too much for her to understand. She repeated what she knew him to be and left it at that.

She said to him:

> *'Yea, Lord:*
> *I believe that thou art the Christ, the Son of God,*
> *which should come into the world.'* (John 11:27)

When Peter made this same confession early in the ministry of Jesus, he seized the opportunity to declare his purpose to build the church to the point where the gates of hell could not prevail against it.

Now he was poised to prove his assertion that he is the Resurrection and the Life.

Martha left and told Mary that the Master was calling her.

As soon as she heard this she left the house quickly and went to see him.

When the Jews in the house saw Mary leave hastily they followed her thinking she was going to the grave to weep there.

Mary came to where Jesus was and fell at his feet saying unto him,

> *'Lord, if thou hadst been here, my brother had not died.'*　　　　　　　　　　　　　　　　(John 11:32)

This was exactly what Martha had said earlier.

The disciples were watching all this with confused amazement. The sadness of the bereaved must have got through to them. But they were puzzled as to what Jesus would do at this time now that Lazarus had been in the grave for four days.

When Jesus heard and saw the crowd of Jews weeping behind Mary he groaned in the spirit, very clearly troubled now.

He asked them where they laid him. As they proceeded to the site the apostle John then recorded the shortest verse in the Bible;

> *'Jesus wept.'*　　　　　　　　　　　　　　　　　　(John 11:35)

He was not weeping out of helplessness or weakness since he had the power to raise Lazarus from the dead. He wept because man that had been made in the image of God had fallen through sin to the place where he had become a prisoner of death.

At the grave which a cave he commanded the people to roll away the stone. Martha kept pleading that her brother had been dead four days and would now be stinking. When the stone was rolled away Jesus lifted up his eyes and said.

> *'Father, I thank thee that thou hast heard me.*
> *And I knew that thou hearest me always:*
> *but because of the people which stand by*
> *I said it, that they may believe that thou hast sent me.'*
> (John 11:41–43)

And when he had thus spoken, he cried with a **loud voice**,

> *'Lazarus, come forth.'* (John 11:43)

The prayer that Jesus prayed had three parts. The first part was thanksgiving, the second part was supplication and the third part was a command by the voice of the Lord.

The voice of the **Lord** has many qualities and is of tremendous power. In Psalm 29 David gives us some descriptions of the voice of the Lord. He tells us:

> *'The voice of the* Lord *is upon the waters:*
> *the God of glory thundereth: the* Lord *is upon many waters.*
> *The voice of the* Lord *is powerful; the voice of the* Lord *is full of majesty.*
> *The voice of the* Lord *breakest the cedars;*
> *Yea, the* Lord *breaketh the cedars of Lebanon.'*
> (Psalm 29:3–5)

In Job 40:9 he asks

> *'Hast thou an arm like God? or canst thou thunder with a voice like him?'*

In the book of the prophet Ezekiel he testifies:

'And when they went, I heard the noise of their wings, like the noise of great waters, as the voice of the Almighty, the voice of speech, as the noise of an host: when they stood, they let down their wings.'

(Ezekiel 1:24)

At that grave side Jesus spoke with the voice of the **Lord**. That voice travelled to the outermost limit of the land of the living and went into the realm of the righteous dead, which were before the death of Jesus staying in a place called Abraham's bosom (Luke 16:22). The voice of the **Lord** located the spirit and soul of Lazarus and took hold of them. They rushed back to Bethany into that grave and into the lifeless body of Lazarus. When they got there the voice of the Lord moved the spirit and soul back into the body and then recreated the body cells, organs and systems of Lazarus.

At the quick completion of this job it pushed the prone horizontal and bound body of Lazarus to the vertical position and propelled him forward to the mouth of the grave still bound with grave clothes.

Jesus then spoke again to say, *'Loose him and let him go.'* The voice of the Lord raised Lazarus. The people who gathered were amazed and the news went all through the land.

Today you can experience the power of the same Jesus who raised Lazarus from the dead. The same Jesus speaking today by the power of the Holy Spirit can bring his power to bear on your life and your circumstances. All things are possible to him that believeth.

Chapter 8

Jesus Commends the Faith of Two Gentiles

Jesus was forthright in his earthly ministry whenever people came to him in their need for help. It was only when people like the Pharisees and the Scribes came with wicked thoughts in their hearts asking questions meant to trap him that he exposed their wickedness by his answers. He was compassionate in dealing with children, women and men. Most of the time the people who came to him were Jews. They were sons and daughters of Abraham and he had been sent first to the lost sheep of Israel.

But on at least two recorded occasions Gentiles who were temporarily not included in the ministry of Jesus (until later) came to him for help. Their encounters with Jesus are worthy of deep study and would be of great help to grasp a little more about Jesus.

The Gentile Woman

> 'Then Jesus went thence, and departed into the coasts of Tyre and Sidon.
> And, behold, a woman of Canaan came out of the same coasts, and cried unto him, saying, Have mercy on me, O Lord, thou Son of David; my daughter is grievously vexed with a devil.'   (Matthew 15:21–22)

This woman's problem was that her daughter was seriously troubled by a devil. Some people may think this was a figment of her imagination, but devils are real and they trouble people in multitudes of ways. They can oppress, depress, obsess and possess people. They can do more. These devils are Satan's foot soldiers who execute his plans in people's lives.

This woman must have heard about Jesus and that he had power to and actually did, cast out devils by his word from people's bodies. Unfortunately she adopted the wrong approach. In addition to the fact that it was not yet time for the Gentiles, she called Jesus as only a Jew at that time was entitled to call him.

She addressed him as Son of David thus creating an impression that she was a Jewess. She was not and therefore not an heiress to the covenant of Abraham with God.

> *'But he answered her not a word.*
> *And his disciples came and besought him,*
> *saying, Send her away; for she crieth after us.'*
> (Matthew 15:23)

She ran into a wall of silence. Jesus did not say anything to her. And for somebody who had such a problem it must have been very saddening. She must have thought about the monumental problems her daughter's condition presented. Whenever the problem started, the distress would be multiplied by two – daughter and mother in anguish. She would have remembered the medical bills, the stares of the neighbours and perhaps the sneering remarks made by some of them. She became desperate and began to appeal to the disciples to help her talk to Jesus.

Since Jesus the Master was silent and she was desperately appealing to them they felt torn by her state.

Rather than send her away themselves they besought Jesus to do so. They wanted him to be aware of her persistence and take a final decisive action.

> *'But he answered and said, I am not sent but unto the*
> *lost sheep of the house of Israel.'* (Matthew 15:24)

In answer to the appeal of his disciples Jesus explained that he was only, as at then, sent to the lost sheep of Israel.

This answer could have deflated her faith and sent her home weeping with her problem unresolved.

Yet she believed and knew that Jesus had the power to end her daughter's terrible affliction. Rather than give up, now that he had spoken to her, she persisted. She refused to believe that the magnitude of his power would only be for the Jews.

> *'Then came she and worshipped him,*
> *saying, Lord, help me.'* (Matthew 15:25)

This woman was dogged in her faith. Rather than go away she came forward and worshipped him pleading at the same time that he help her.

The tension here must have been quite high with the woman refusing to take 'No' for an answer. Yet it appeared she was not getting anywhere.

> *'But he answered and said, It is not meet to take the children's bread, and to cast it to dogs.'*
> (Matthew 15:26)

The woman could easily have either taken offence here at being implicitly called a dog, or been overtaken with self pity at having tried so hard yet apparently failing. Yet she chose to hear that the meat was available. Because her faith was unshakeable even in the face of this word that appeared to exclude her, she quickly seized on an opening which only those with desperate faith can see.

> *'And she said, Truth, Lord: yet the dogs eat of the crumbs which fall from their masters' table.'*
> (Matthew 15:27)

This reminds me of the testimony of a converted armed

robber turned preacher given at a Regional Convention of the FGBMFI in Uyo, Nigeria in 1992. He was born again while in prison awaiting trial. At the trial he pleaded guilty and called no witnesses. While awaiting judgement he prayed to God to be saved from the gallows. The Lord spoke to him and said that by the law of God, the law of the country and the law of nature, anybody who killed another person would die. And that having been forgiven of his sin he would go to heaven after execution. Then he asked God whether the scripture that says *'With God nothing shall be impossible'* applied to his case.

According to him the Lord intervened and he was set free on the judgement day and is now serving the Lord. There was hardly a dry eye left in the convention hall the day he shared his testimony. You could feel the powerful compassion of God in a hopeless situation.

This woman had seized an opening in the statement of Jesus. In addition to her faith she showed meekness. She did not mind belonging to the class of dogs but then pointed out that the dogs ate the crumbs that fell from the table. The crumbs were of the same substance as the children would have eaten at the table but had advertently or inadvertently been thrown from there. Nobody usually quarrelled with the dogs for eating the crumbs. Those were their portion.

> *'Then Jesus answered and said unto her, O woman, great is thy faith: be it unto thee even as thou wilt. And her daughter was made whole from that very hour.'*
> (Matthew 15:28)

Jesus, clearly impressed and moved by this woman's faith, first of all commends her, *'O woman, great is thy faith.'*

That commendation has entered God's eternal records. The Syro-Phoenician woman had become an everlasting example of a possessor of great faith.

But more immediately Jesus gave her what she had

been pressing for. His words of power were uttered. The daughter was made whole from that very hour.

This woman by her faith gate crashed into the blessings of the Jews. She enjoyed the blessings of a dispensation earlier than her own. A woman of great faith indeed.

The Believing Centurion

> *'And when Jesus was entered into Capernaum, there came unto him a centurion, beseeching him,*
> *And saying, Lord, my servant lieth at home sick of the palsy, grievously tormented.*
> *And Jesus saith unto him, I will come and heal him.'*
>
> (Matthew 8:5–7)

In this case the centurion came on behalf of his servant who was grievously tormented. In addition this servant was sick of the palsy; in other words a paralytic. Jesus agreed to come and heal the servant. Ordinarily the story would have ended there but the centurion supplied a new dimension to the story.

> *'The centurion answered and said, Lord, I am not worthy that thou shouldest come under my roof: but speak the word only, and my servant shall be healed.*
> *For I am under authority, having soldiers under me: and I say to this man, Go, and he goeth; and to another, Come, and he cometh; and to my servant, Do this, and he doeth it.'*
>
> (Matthew 8:8–9)

This Roman army officer understood the ministry of Jesus from the perspective of the military. He must have seen that Jesus had authority and that his words carried spiritual power. He must have been so awed and humbled by this immense spiritual power that even though he was an officer in the colonial occupation army, he felt so small that he felt Jesus was too big to come to his house. It appears that great faith should go hand in hand with humility. He must have thought about this very clearly. His servant's problem touched him.

One could see another side of the officer's character. Even though he could have disposed of this servant and taken up another one, yet he did not do so.

In fact there was no guarantee that Jesus would not deliver a public snub to him by refusing to do anything, yet he took that risk.

It is touching to see such a high official take such a risk on behalf of a helpless servant. That is real and true compassion. The centurion's answer to Jesus showed that he understood the difference between natural and spiritual authority. His authority as an officer could move men but was nothing in the realm of moving spirits.

But he saw that the authority which Jesus had could deal with spirits and the natural. It transcended both worlds.

Whereas the Jewish leaders spent their time questioning the authority of Jesus, scheming and planning how to trap him with their little minds and framing ridiculous questions with their puny intellect, this Roman officer clearly understood that Jesus was no ordinary man. Even though he carried Caesar's commission as a captain yet he was prepared to bow before the superior authority of Jesus.

His statement – *'Just speak the word only, and my servant shall be healed'* is a classic in the study of faith. It left no room for doubt and portrayed his absolute and imperative belief in the person and power of Jesus.

> *'When Jesus heard it, he marvelled, and said to them that followed, Verily I say unto you, I have not found so great faith, no, not in Israel.*
> *And I say unto you, That many shall come from the east and west, and shall sit down with Abraham, and Isaac, and Jacob, in the Kingdom of heaven.*
> *But the children of the Kingdom shall be cast out into outer darkness: there shall be weeping and gnashing of teeth.'* (Matthew 8:10–12)

The effect of this Gentile centurion's faith was to make Jesus marvel. He then took the opportunity to commend the centurion stating he had not seen such faith in Israel. What a compliment.

It would appear that this officer had more faith than the disciples, the Scribes and the Pharisees. He certainly had more faith than Thomas Didymus. Being a forthright and true Teacher, Jesus spoke this compliment to all who followed to challenge them to wake up. When He now spoke about outsiders sitting with the patriarchs in the Kingdom while the children of the Kingdom *'languished outside'* it was a warning that the Kingdom of heaven is not for any presumptuous people but for those who qualify on the merit of their faith and conduct.

Listening to all this the centurion must have felt he was getting more than he bargained for. He had come to beseech Jesus on behalf of his servant and now Jesus was talking about seating in the Kingdom of heaven.

It is important here to note that whatever brings you near to Jesus, his ultimate aim is that we qualify to sit with him in his throne in heaven.

> *'And Jesus said unto the centurion, Go thy way; and as thou hast believed, so be it done unto thee. And his servant was healed in the self same hour.'*
>
> (Matthew 8:13)

Jesus again spoke the word of power and healing. The centurion was given the word he came for. The moment those words were spoken his servant at home was healed. The word of the Lord had travelled from the scene of the encounter to the sick man in the house releasing him from the bondage of the palsy and from the grips of the spirits that had grievously troubled him.

There is no distance in the spiritual realm.

The words of Jesus can traverse any distance and bring healing to our needs.

Chapter 9

Jesus the Builder of
the Church

One of the major reasons why Jesus came into the world was to call out a body of people who would receive him and believe in him. These people would then be the vessels through which his character and purpose would be made manifest to the world and to the powers of darkness.

It is a difficult thing to say but it is very true that most people do not know who actually owns the Church. Again there is a lot of ignorance about the purposes of the Church. This kind of ignorance plays into the hands of the Kingdom of darkness which seizes the opportunity to its own advantage.

Jesus waited for an opportune time to broach the subject of the Church to his disciples and he went about it as usual in a most interesting way.

> 'When Jesus came into the coasts of Caesarea Philippi, he asked his disciples, saying, Whom do men say that I the Son of man am? And they said, Some say that thou art John the Baptist: some, Elias; and others Jeremias, or one of the prophets.
> He saith unto them, But whom say ye that I am?
> And Simon Peter answered and said, Thou art the Christ, the Son of the living God.

> *And Jesus answered and said unto him, Blessed are thou, Simon Barjona: for flesh and blood hath not revealed it unto thee, but my Father which is in heaven.*
>
> *And I say unto thee, That thou art Peter, and upon this rock I will build my church; and the gates of hell shall not prevail against it.*
>
> *And I will give unto thee the keys of the Kingdom of heaven: and whatsoever thou shalt bind on earth shall be bound in heaven: and whatsoever thou shalt loose on earth shall be loosed in heaven.'*

(Matthew 16:13–19)

This discussion throws a number of very crucial facts into focus. First of all no one can know the Lord Jesus unless God the Father reveals him to such a person. It is not possible to know Jesus intellectually or through reason except by revelation.

When one does not know Jesus personally he cannot know anything about the Church, not being a part of it. The Church is a dynamic organism and not an organisation. It is being built by Jesus Christ its founder and owner to be an instrument of spiritual violence against the Kingdom of darkness – the gates of hell. Jesus plans that the Church will be so strong that the Kingdom of darkness will not stand before her.

Furthermore to enable the church perform this feat he is giving her the keys of the kingdom – authority.

When the Church exercises this authority, whatever she binds on earth is bound in heaven and whatever she looses on earth is loosed in heaven.

The Church should be what Jesus the Builder intends it to be not what the ideas of theologians or even the cultures of men want it to be.

Knowing Jesus is the key. Knowing the Holy Spirit whose ministry is to progressively reveal Jesus ensures that we keep in touch. Jesus, quite a few times in the book of Revelation kept saying:

> '*He who has an ear, let him hear what the Spirit says to the churches.*' (Revelation 2:7 NKJV)

A reading of the New Testament will always reveal each time around something new about what Jesus plans for the Church.

In 1 Peter 2:5, 9–10 the Holy Spirit gives a very clear picture of some aspects of the Church that Jesus is building.

> '*Ye also, as lively stones, are built up a spiritual house, an holy priesthood, to offer up spiritual sacrifices, acceptable to God by Jesus Christ.*
> *But ye are a chosen generation, a royal priesthood an holy nation, a peculiar people; that ye should shew forth the praises of him who hath called you out of darkness into his marvellous light:*
> *Which in time past were not a people, but are now the people of God: which had not obtained mercy, but now have obtained mercy.*'

The Church is made up of lively stones being built up into a spiritual house through the work of the Holy Spirit. The Church should be offering spiritual sacrifices acceptable to God.

The first sacrifice that each person has to offer is their body.

> '*I beseech you therefore, brethren, by the mercies of God, that ye present your bodies a living sacrifice, holy, acceptable unto God, which is your reasonable service.*' (Romans 12:1)

The reasons for demanding this sacrifice from every believer are manifold but it is important to mention two of the most cogent because they mark the difference between believers and unbelievers.

The Church '*ekklesia*' is made up of believers in Christ,

not people who go through rituals of religious observances and ceremonies. The first reason is that each believer is God's temple. God dwells in each believer by the Holy Spirit.

> *'Know ye not that ye are the temple of God and that the Spirit of God dwelleth in you?*
> *If any man defile the temple of God, him shall God destroy; for the temple of God is holy, which temple ye are.'* (1 Corinthians 3:16–17)

The second reason is that each believer is bought with a price – the blood of Jesus Christ which is so precious that it cannot be quantified in terms of money.

> *'What? know ye not that your body is the temple of the Holy Ghost which is in you, which ye have of God, and ye are not your own?*
> *For ye are bought with a price: therefore glorify God in your body, and in your spirit, which are God's.'*
> (1 Corinthians 6:19–20)

Believers are kings and priests. By their lifestyles and character it should be seen that they are a peculiar people and a holy nation. One of their primary callings is to show forth the glory of Jesus Christ who has called them out of darkness into his marvellous light.

A conclusion that can be drawn thus far from the abundant evidence of Scripture is that Christianity is not religious rituals but a life of walking with God in devotion to his will.

Marriages

One other thing that should mark believers out from the rest of the world is the quality of marriage.

Marriages abound all over the world. People of all races, creeds and levels of life marry, and from available statistics the failure rate is very high. People endure it, tough it out or merely do not try at all.

But for believers the pattern is clearly taught all over Scripture. It is important that the pattern and order are adhered to because the picture of the relationship between Christ and the Church is that of a man and his wife.

> *'Wives, submit yourselves unto your own husbands, as unto the Lord.*
>
> *For the husband is the head of the wife, even as Christ is the head of the church:*
>
> *and he is the saviour of the body.*
>
> *Therefore as the church is subject unto Christ, so let the wives be to their own husbands in everything.*
>
> *Husbands, love your wives, even as Christ also loved the church, and gave himself for it;*
>
> *... For this cause shall a man leave his father and mother, and shall be joined unto his wife, and they two shall be one flesh.*
>
> *This is a great mystery: but I speak concerning Christ and the church.*
>
> *Nevertheless let every one of you in particular so love his wife even as himself; and the wife see that she reverence her husband.'*   (Ephesians 5:22–25, 31–33)

When these commandments are kept marriage is enjoyable, almost heavenly. God can cause such marriages to do much work to glorify his name and to help people. God's order in marriage points to the fact that it is not just an institution but one in which government is involved. The man is the head with the responsibilities to love the wife as Christ loved the Church and gave himself for it. He is to cherish her, nourish her, provide for her and cover her.

The wife is to obey, reverence, honour and love the husband.

Everyone would be well advised to seek the help of the

Holy Spirit to attain unto God's standard in marriage. Jesus promised us that when the Holy Spirit comes he would teach us **all things** and this includes marriage. Furthermore in 1 Corinthians 2:10–12 we are told:

> '... *For the Spirit searches all things, yea, the deep things of God. For what man knoweth the things of a man, save the Spirit of man which is in him? even so the things of God knoweth no man, but the Spirit of God.*
>
> *Now we have received, not the spirit of the world, but the spirit which is of God, that we might know the things that are freely given to us of God.*'

Married people should seriously seek the help of the Holy Spirit in marriage. It is not an institution established by man but by God. It is a spiritual union of two people and to be able to succeed in it we need the help of the Holy Spirit to help us understand it, go through it and achieve the purposes God has for it so that we will be rewarded by him.

In Revelation 2 and 3 Jesus dictated letters to each of the seven churches of Asia. As early as when John the Apostle was still alive the Church had begun going astray through disobedience and heresies.

However when we read the letters to the churches in Ephesus, Smyrna, Pergamos, Thyatira, Sardis, Philadelphia and Laodicea we discover that Jesus wants, and will not compromise his desire for, a perfect Church.

In each church he makes detailed observations of their strengths and weaknesses and bluntly warns about what must be done or alternatively they would face judgment.

Those observations and warnings are still valid till today and we need to take them to heart because we are the generation upon whom the ends of the world are come. To the church at Ephesus he warned

> 'Nevertheless I have somewhat against thee, because thou hast left thy first love.

> *Remember therefore from whence thou art fallen, and repent, and do the first works; or else I will come unto thee quickly, and will remove thy candlestick out of his place, except thou repent.'* (Revelation 2:4–5)

Have you left your first love? Then repent and do the first works.

The church at Smyrna was troubled by the blasphemy of those who belonged to the synagogue of Satan. The church there faced tremendous persecution, tribulation and imprisonment.

The church at Pergamos had people in it who were holding the doctrine of Balaam in encouraging people to commit fornication and to eat things sacrificed to idols. There were also people who held the doctrine of the Nicolaitans. They were warned to repent quickly or the Lord would come to fight against them with the sword of his mouth.

In Thyatira the problem was that they had a woman, Jezebel, who called herself a prophetess and her ministry was to teach and seduce the Lord's servants to commit fornication and to eat things sacrificed to idols.

In Sardis they had a name depicting them as living but were in fact dead. Their works were not found perfect before God. The Lord Jesus Christ warned:

> *'Be watchful, and strengthen the things which remain, that are ready to die.*
> *...Remember therefore how thou hast received and heard, and hold fast, and repent.'* (Revelation 3:2–3)

There was no fault found with the church in Philadelphia.

And in Laodicea the problem was that they were neither cold nor hot, but lukewarm. They said they were rich, increased in goods and had need of nothing. Unfortunately they did not know that they were wretched, miserable, and poor, and blind and naked.

The Lord Jesus Christ counselled them to buy of him gold tried in the fire, white raiment and eye salve.

To make matters worse still they had locked the Lord Jesus Christ out of their church and he was now standing at the door knocking. If anyone heard his voice and opened the door he would come in and sup with such a person.

The question is: how are we in our standing with the Lord Jesus Christ? Is there anything we know is wrong? Has he in any way indicted us? Time is running out. The call is for repentance and returning to the first works.

Chapter 10

The Sufferings and Death of Jesus

'Who hath believed our report? and to whom is the arm of the LORD revealed?
For he shall grow up before him as a tender plant, and as a root out of a dry ground: he hath no form nor comeliness; and when we shall see him there is no beauty that we should desire him.
He is despised and rejected of men; a man of sorrows, and acquainted with grief: and we hid as it were our faces from him; he was despised, and we esteemed him not.
Surely he hath borne our griefs, and carried our sorrows: yet we did esteem him stricken, smitten of God, and afflicted.
But he was wounded for our transgressions, he was bruised for our iniquities: the chastisement of our peace was upon him; and with his stripes we are healed.'　　　　　　　　　　(Isaiah 53:1–5)

This very moving passage from the prophecy of Isaiah gives us a summary of the sufferings of Jesus Christ on our behalf. The whole chapter describes various aspects of his passion and death. If we can but begin to understand the different ways in which he suffered and what each provided for us, it would enormously strengthen our faith and kindle even more gratitude and loyalty towards him.

1. His Betrayal

It is very deeply instructive that one of his twelve disciples, indeed the one entrusted with carrying the money for the group, would be so greedy as to contemplate selling Jesus to the Jewish leaders. Three and half years of walking with Jesus, seeing his miracles and listening to his profound teaching did not deeply affect Judas Iscariot. All he cared about was money. He forgot that no one can serve God and mammon. Even the rebuke from Jesus when Mary broke the alabaster box of ointment to anoint the master's feet did not change his priorities.

> *'Then one of the twelve, called Judas Iscariot, went unto the chief priests, And said unto them, What will ye give me, and I will deliver him unto you? And they covenanted with him for thirty pieces of silver.*
> *And from that time he sought opportunity to betray him.'* (Matthew 26:14–16)

Judas preferred what he would be given – money, to him who came to seek and to save that which was lost. Thirty pieces of silver, a remarkable sum of money, was enough to tune his heart to the frequency where he now was no longer interested in Jesus as a person, but sought opportunity to betray him. A very perverse and wicked preoccupation for a man's heart.

> *'And while he yet spake, lo, Judas, one of the twelve, came, and with him a great multitude with swords and staves, from the chief priests and elders of the people. Now he that betrayed him gave them a sign, saying, whomsoever I shall kiss, that same is he: hold him fast. And forthwith he came to Jesus, and said, Hail, master; and kissed him.*
> *And Jesus said unto him, Friend, wherefore art thou come?*
> *Then came they, and laid hands on Jesus, and took him.'* (Matthew 26:47–50)

Judas had worked his heinous plan to perfection. Jesus had known all along that it would be Judas, and mentioned, while they were eating the Last Supper, that one of the disciples would betray him. After the disciples had each asked, 'Is it I?', Jesus said it were better for that man if he had not been born!

His betrayal has some very significant things about it. Firstly, Jesus was given into the hands of the chief priests. Secondly, he lost albeit, his personal liberty. Thirdly, he was sold for 30 pieces of silver. The money is described in Matthew 27:6 as *'the price of blood'* – in other words, **Blood money**. Furthermore, the piece of land it was eventually used to buy was called, *'The field of blood'*, (v. 8).

By this betrayal for 30 pieces of silver, Jesus paid the price for the sin of **slavery**. He also paid the price of the indignity and debasement of those affected by the scourge of slavery.

Slavery is a heinous sin punishable with death.

> *'And he that stealeth a man, and selleth him, or if he be found in his hand, he shall surely be put to death.'*
> (Exodus 21:16)

The same law was reiterated in Deuteronomy 24:7, namely kidnapping and slavery. It is even more significant that the highest amount of damages due to the owner of a slave if the slave was killed by an ox in an accident, was thirty pieces of silver (Exodus 21:32).

This same amount was prophetic as we see from the book of Zechariah 11:12, 13 where a direct reference was made to it.

In ministering deliverance to those tainted by slavery, the mention of the thirty pieces of silver, by which Jesus purchased their liberty, has a very powerful effect in forcing Satan to loose them spiritually because he still legally considers them chattels and still insists on seeing them with manacles round their hands and feet and with chains around their necks.

2. The Crown of Thorns

> '*And when they had plaited a crown of thorns, they put it upon his head, and a reed in his right hand: and they bowed the knee before him, and mocked him, saying, Hail, King of the Jews!'*   (Matthew 27:29)

The soldiers who were part of Pilate's guard and who formed part of the garrison of Jerusalem, played a significant role in the sufferings of Jesus. One of the things they did was to plait a crown of thorns and jam it on the head of Jesus. It must have been indescribably painful! In enduring this, Jesus was paying for the curse which God put upon the ground, in Genesis, as a result of man's sin.

> '*And unto Adam he said, Because thou has hearkened unto the voice of thy wife, and hast eaten of the tree, of which I commanded thee, saying, Thou shall not eat it: cursed is the ground for thy sake; in sorrow shalt thou eat of it all the days of thy life;*
> *Thorns also and thistles shall it bring forth to thee; and thou shalt eat of the herb of the field;'*
> (Genesis 3:17–18)

This aspect of Jesus's sufferings needs to be understood in breaking curses upon the ground. In dealing with the ground, whether for farming, building, or any other purpose, this fact needs to be used. Satan needs to be told that the curse upon the ground has been paid for, so he must relinquish his hold upon it.

3. His Stripes

> '*. . . and with his stripes we are healed.'*   (Isaiah 53:5)

The prophet spoke of the stripes with which Jesus would be beaten. Soldiers are a rough set of men and when they are authorised to be brutal by a person in authority, they really are brutal. Pilate delivered Jesus to them to be scourged.

> *'Then released he Barabbas unto them: and when he had scourged Jesus, he delivered him to be crucified.'*
> (Matthew 27:26)

By Roman law, the number of lashes to be administered was thirty-nine. The soldiers did a terrible job with this task. Roman scourges, or whips, had a handle much like a tobacco head and strands of leather with pieces of bone or metal at the ends to inflict maximum injury. A picture of what happened is gleaned from the prophetic word which David spoke:

> *'The plowers plowed upon my back: they made long their furrows.'* (Psalm 129:3)

By the time the beatings and the crown of thorns had taken their toll, we get the picture spoken of by Isaiah.

> *'As many were astonished at thee: his visage was so marred more than any man, and his form more than the sons of men:'* (Isaiah 52:14)

Taking all of these together, we come to the conclusion that Jesus was so badly battered that no artist could ever paint any picture on canvas to give us an idea of what he must have looked like. If his form was marred more than the sons of men, then artists can take a rest from their speculations.

He was beaten to pay for our healing.

> *'Who his own self bare our sins in his body on the tree, that we, being dead to sins, should live unto righteousness; by whose stripes ye were healed.'*
> (1 Peter 2:24)

4. *Hunger, Thirst, Nakedness and Want of All Things*

Jesus suffered many significant things which ought to be noted and the benefits therefrom appropriated. In Deuteronomy 28:48 we read the summary of the curse of poverty:

> *'Therefore shalt thou serve thine enemies which the Lord shall send against thee, in hunger, and in thirst, and in nakedness, and in want of all things: and he shall put a yoke of iron upon they neck, until he have destroyed thee.'* (Deuteronomy 28:48)

Let us first note that from the last supper until he rose from the dead, Jesus did not eat anything. He was hungry throughout the trials, scourging, the crucifixion, and of course in the grave. He was hungry. Secondly, he was thirsty.

> *'After this, Jesus knowing that all things were now accomplished, that the scripture might be fulfilled, saith, I thirst.'* (John 19:28)

Even when a soldier offered vinegar on a sponge he refused to take it, either to deaden the pain he was suffering or even to soothe his throat.

Thirdly, he was stripped naked in that his garments were taken from him and the soldiers gambled for them at the foot of the cross.

> *'And they crucified him, and parted his garments, casting lots: that it might be fulfilled which was spoken by the prophet, They parted my garments among them, and upon my vesture did they cast lots.'*
>
> (Matthew 27:35)

Finally when he gave up the ghost, he had no personal sepulchre in which to be buried. Joseph of Arimathaea surrendered his own personal sepulchre for Jesus to be buried in.

> *'When the even was come, there came a rich man of Arimathaea, named Joseph, who also himself was Jesus' disciple: He went to Pilate, and begged for the body of Jesus. Then Pilate commanded the body to be delivered.*
> *And when Joseph had taken the body, he wrapped it in a clean linen cloth.*
> *And laid it in his own new tomb, which he had hewn out in the rock: and he rolled a great stone to the door of the sepulchre, and departed.'*
>
> (Matthew 27:57–60)

In his death Jesus was hungry, thirsty, naked and in want of all things including a tomb in which to be buried, thereby paying the price for the curse of poverty. This can also be appropriated by faith as part of the benefits from his sufferings.

Chapter 11

Jesus On the Cross

Jesus was crucified on a cross on Mount Calvary in the place called Golgotha. God chose this mode of death for him for very specific reasons. He could have been stoned to death like Stephen, beheaded like John the Baptist, or strangled. Jesus was crucified because he had to be made a curse for us.

> *'Christ hath redeemed us from the curse of the law, being made a curse for us: for it is written, Cursed is every one that hangeth on a tree:*
> *That the blessing of Abraham might come on the Gentiles through Jesus Christ; that we might receive the promise of the Spirit through faith.'*
>
> (Galatians 3:13, 14)

Two other reasons appear from the same scripture. If Jesus had not died on the cross, the blessing of Abraham could never have come on the Gentiles. Furthermore, the promise of the Spirit which Jesus made, could only reach us because he died on the cross. Therefore to escape the limitations of curses, to receive the blessing of Abraham and to receive the promise of the Spirit, we claim them by virtue of his death on the Cross.

Jesus hung on that Cross for six hours. While he was suspended between heaven and earth certain miracles took place.

74

The Darkness

> *'Now from the sixth hour there was darkness all over the land unto the ninth hour.'* (Matthew 27:45)

This darkness was a manifestation of the effect of man's sin on creation. It also covered certain aspects of his suffering on the cross. This darkness was remarkable.

The Veil

> *'Jesus, when he had cried again with a loud voice, yielded up the ghost.*
> *And, behold, the veil of the temple was rent in twain from the top to the bottom; . . .'* (Matthew 27:50–51)

The veil of the temple covered the entrance into the Holiest of All, into which only the High Priest entered once a year. Inside, there was the ark, and the glory of God showing his Presence. No ordinary person could see, or go inside there. Thus was God separated from the children of Israel.

The death of Jesus coincided with the hour when the priests must have been preparing to slaughter the passover Lamb, and the sudden rending of the veil must have startled and shocked the priests. Thus did God dispose of their services and summarily end the offering of the animals when that perfect sacrifice had been offered on the cross.

The Earthquake

> *'. . . and the earth did quake . . .'* (Matthew 27:51)

The earthquake was remarkable in that it could not pull down the cross nor the man on it. Some authors have said that the earth could not drink the blood of its Creator without convulsing.

The Graves Opened

> '... *And the graves were opened*...'
>
> (Matthew 27:52)

This was no ordinary event. Without hands or any digging implements being used, graves opened! This is a foretaste or rehearsal of what will happen at the Rapture. It also shows that the death of Jesus on the Cross affected the region under the earth.

Resurrection of the Saints

> '... *and many bodies of the saints which slept arose. And came out of the graves after his resurrection, and went into the holy city, and appeared unto many.*'
>
> (Matthew 27:52–53)

This is very remarkable. The saints who had been all the time in the place called 'Abraham's bosom', were then resurrected, because the supreme sacrifice of Jesus shedding his Blood had been paid. This is a definite foretaste of what will happen to the dead in Christ at the Rapture when they shall come out of their graves and be caught up to meet him in the clouds. Jesus had tasted death and not only overcome it but destroyed the power of him who had power over death, that is, the devil.

Salvation of the Thief on the Cross

> '*And one of the malefactors which were hanged railed on him, saying, If thou be Christ, save thyself and us. But the other answering rebuked him, saying, Dost not thou fear God, seeing thou art in the same condemnation?*
>
> *And we indeed justly; for we receive the due reward of our deeds: but this man hath done nothing amiss.*
>
> *And he said unto Jesus, Lord, remember me when thou comest into thy kingdom.*

And Jesus said unto him, Verily I say unto thee, Today shalt thou be with me in paradise.'

(Luke 23:39–43)

The two thieves on their crosses had a date with destiny, being crucified with Jesus on the same day, in the same place and at the same hour.

The words of the first, show him to be an ignorant and unrepentant sinner but the second thief had come to his senses and acknowledged that he was receiving just punishment for his deeds. He went further in acknowledging that Jesus was guiltless, and repentantly pleaded that Jesus should remember him when he would come into his kingdom. He recognised Jesus as Lord and understood that he had a kingdom. He was however ignorant on one point: if Jesus were to wait until he entered his Kingdom before remembering him, it would be too late, so Jesus pronounced the word of salvation there and then on the cross.

We see that Jesus did not lose his power to save, even on the cross. He tasted death, paid the price for sin, was made a curse, was made sin for us, and overcame principalities and powers, making a public show of them and triumphing over them all on that cross.

The cross and the events which took place on it are inescapably central to our salvation, and no one can truly know Jesus Christ except such a person accepts and appropriates the work he did on that cross.

The events which took place were so dramatic and tremendous that another miracle happened.

Confession of the Roman Centurion

'And when the centurion, which stood over against him, saw that he so cried out, and gave up the ghost, he said. Truly this man was the Son of God.'

(Mark 15:39)

The centurion who was in charge of the execution squad had watched all the strange things happening. His spirit was moved to make this great confession. The door to the heart of this Roman, battle-hardened centurion was opened to acknowledge Jesus as the Son of God. What a mighty miracle!

Chapter 12

The Blood of His Cross

*'And, having made peace through the blood of his cross, by him to reconcile **all things** unto himself; by him, I say, whether they be things in earth, or things in heaven.*
***And you**, that were sometime alienated and enemies in your mind by wicked works, yet now hath he reconciled.*
In the body of his flesh through death, to present you holy and unblameable and unreproveable in his sight;'
(Colossians 1:20–22)

The blood which Jesus shed on the cross bought for us, and gave us, eternal benefits and blessings.

Peace

He made peace between us and God by that blood. We who were enemies of God by wicked works, now have peace with God.

Reconciliation

After making peace when a quarrel is settled, the atmosphere between the parties could be frosty, cold, formal, or even worse. One party could still feel cheated. But Jesus, by his blood, went further to reconcile us men to himself and to God by his blood.

Reconciling All Things

This is one vital aspect which many people miss. Jesus did not only shed his blood for men: He shed his blood to reconcile **all things**, whether they be things in earth or things in heaven. There are two wide aspects to this – firstly all things on earth which had rebelled and are groaning as a result of man's sin, rebellion and fall, have been reconciled.

The believers can, by prayer and prophetic action, enable them to enjoy this reconciliation. For example you can pray over your plants, fruit trees, livestock and the power of God will touch them.

Again, certain things in heaven were affected by man's sin. Those things were reconciled by the blood of Jesus, to God.

Forgiveness of Sins

> *'In whom we have redemption through his blood, the forgiveness of sins, according to the riches of his grace.'* (Ephesians 1:7)

The blood of Jesus procured for us forgiveness of our sins. It is perhaps necessary to think of, and remember, that such heinous sins as murder, fornication, adultery, lying, abortion, drunkenness, covetousness, lasciviousness, homosexuality, hatred, malice, witchcraft, sorcery, necromancy, masturbation, stealing and others are forgiven because of the blood of Jesus, providing we repent and indulge no more in them.

Redemption

The blood of Jesus affords us redemption. The meaning of redemption is threefold. A combination of the three levels of meaning gives us a good understanding of that wonderful word.

To understand it we need to look very briefly at the three

Greek words that explain it. The first is *'agorazo'*, meaning to buy. The second word is *'exagorazo'* meaning to buy out, especially of purchasing a slave with a view to his freedom (Vine's N.T. Dictionary). The third word is *'lutroo'* meaning to release, to set free on receipt of the ransom.

We need to therefore understand that the blood of Jesus obtained these three levels of legal status and we need to experience them empirically and teach others so. The blood of Jesus has paid the price for our sin, bought us out of the slave market and loosed us from the clutches, claims and the calamities of sin. Deliverance from inherited sinful family traits can be obtained, and demons which bind people in specific sins can now be cast out so that people can be fully released.

Pleading the blood of Jesus can be used to decode whatever Satan has programmed into peoples genes, and to destroy them by authoritative prayer, so that family sins are uprooted from their lives. This is important when you realize that in the family line of Judah, he committed incest with his daughter-in-law in Genesis 38. Ten generations (Matthew 1:1–6) later David committed adultery (2 Samuel 11). His first son Amnon raped his half-sister Tamar (2 Samuel 13:14). Another son, Absalom, slept with ten of his father's wives (2 Samuel 16:21–22), Adonijah, another son, desired his father's wife Abishag and was beheaded for it. Then finally Solomon, who succeeded David, married 1000 women altogether (1 Kings 11:1–3).

We see here eleven generations in one family falling prey to the spirit of immorality manifesting itself in incest, adultery, rape and the unspeakable abomination of a son sleeping with his father's concubines.

Justification

> *'Much more then, being now justified by his blood, we shall be saved from wrath through him.'*
>
> (Romans 5:9)

This is a highly legal blessing. When a person is found guilty he is convicted. All sinners are guilty before God and the sentence is death and damnation in hell, and later in the lake of fire.

But when a convicted person is pardoned by the exercise of executive clemency, or the prerogative of mercy, he can never again be regarded as an 'ex-convict'! He is spoken of and regarded as if the offence were never committed. He is like an acquitted person. So is justification in the case of a believer.

Sanctification

> *'Wherefore Jesus also, that he might sanctify the people with his own blood, suffered without the gate.'*
> (Hebrews 13:12)

The blood of Jesus was shed to sanctify us. This means to set us apart to and for himself. the blood of Jesus therefore makes us separate from the world, and we need to keep it so.

Remission of Sins

> *'. . . and without shedding of blood is no remission.'*
> (Hebrews 9:22)

> *'And their sins and iniquities will I remember no more.*
> *Now where remission of these is, there is no more offering for sin.'*   (Hebrews 10:17–18)

The Greek word translated remission is *'aphesis'* meaning sending away. Our sins were sent away by the blood of Jesus. The second passage quoted above bears out the truth of this assertion. If in truth, our sins have been 'sent away', then there is no more offering for sin as was required under the law of Moses.

The blood of Jesus has provided for us an inexhaustible store of benefits.

Cleansing Us from Sin

> *'But if we walk in the light, as he is in the light, we have fellowship one with another, and the blood of Jesus Christ his Son cleanseth us from all sin.'* (1 John 1:7)

As we walk before the Lord and have fellowship one with another the Lord continually cleanses us by his blood. This goes on in the present continuous tense. One can think of spiritual defilements pollutions and contaminations. There are some sins which one can commit unawares. The blood of Jesus takes care of all these. The word translated 'cleanse' is the Greek work *'katharizo'*, meaning to make clean, to clear. We are made clean and cleared of all sin.

Boldness to Enter into the Holiest

> *'Having therefore, brethren, boldness to enter into the holiest by the blood of Jesus.'* (Hebrews 10:19)

The blood of Jesus gives us boldness to enter into the holiest of all, where the presence of God is experienced.

Now in the New Covenant, believers have access into the place which was sealed off to the people in the Old Testament. Because of the Blood of Jesus we have unimpeded access with boldness before God.

Chapter 13

'It Is Finished'

'When Jesus therefore had received the vinegar, he said, It is finished: and he bowed his head, and gave up the ghost.'   (John 19:30)

When Jesus made that statement, *'It is finished'*, a lot of things were implied. First, the work of man's redemption was finished. The first phase of his work was finished. Everything concerning salvation, healing, baptism, curses, demon possession, and spiritual warfare had now been provided for. Men who received Jesus could now enjoy the finished work in these aspects. The legal provisions were now translatable into empirical experience.

One mistake many believers make is to equate the circumstances with the empirical experience. There are conditions or steps involved in bringing these things into our experience.

We need to enforce them by prayer, by faith, by obedience, by knowledge, by revelation, by the power of the Holy Spirit, by the anointing and by boldness.

He Tasted Death

'Forasmuch then as the children are partakers of flesh and blood, he also himself likewise took part of the same; that through death he might destroy him that had the power of death, that is, the devil.

*And deliver them who through fear of death were all
their lifetime subject to bondage.'* (Hebrews 2:14, 15)

Death is a mysterious phenomenon that has puzzled,
harassed and frightened man from the fall.

Men took all kinds of precautions, but unfortunately
there was no armour against death. It ruled with rigour,
and taunted the human race until Jesus came. Death
struck fear and left sorrow in the hearts of people whenever it visited. It has been called the grim reaper.

Death sounded so final, that when a relative died, the
parting and the consequent heartbreak were the hardest
part to bear, but Jesus came and took death 'head-on',
and overpowered it.

Death could not hold him; He tasted it and took the
sting out of it. In fact, Paul in the Scriptures, enlightens us
further on the subject.

*'Know ye not, that so many of us as were baptized into
Jesus Christ were baptized into his death?
Therefore we are buried with him by baptism into
death; that like as Christ was raised up from the dead
by the glory of the Father, even so we also should walk
in newness of life.'* (Romans 6:3–4)

We partake of his victory over death as we are baptized
into him. As the Holy Spirit baptizes us into Christ at
conversion, and we acknowledge this by water baptism,
we are baptized into his death. Not only did he taste
death, he destroyed the devil. To understand this we need
to look at certain clearer translations of this text Hebrews
2:14(b).

The New Testament, from some of the 26 translations,
has this to say:

*'...that through death he might destroy him ... he
might bring to nought him.'*
(American Standard Version)

85

'...*in order that by death he might render powerless him.*'   (Twentieth Century New Testament)
'...*might put a stop to the power of him.*' (Williams)
'...*so that through death he might break the power of him.*'   (New English Bible)
'...*He might neutralise the one.*'   (Berkeley)
'*In order that by his death he might dethrone.*'

(Goodspeed)

'...*He might paralyze him.*'   (Rotherham)
'...*so that by dying he might crush him.*'   (Moffatt)
'...*that had the power of death, that is the devil; that held the dominion of death, that is the Adversary.*'

(Rotherham)

'...*Whose power lies in death – that is the devil.*'
(Twentieth Century New Testament)
'...*Who had authority over death.*'   (Weymouth)
'...*who wields the power of death.*'   (Moffatt)
'...*who had death at his command.*'

(New English Bible)

'...*the lord of death, that is the devil.*'

(Confraternity)

These various translations clearly give us the understanding that Satan, the Devil was crushed, dethroned, paralysed, rendered powerless and defeated. The victory over Satan was settled.

He Blotted Out the Handwriting of Ordinances Which was Against Us

'*And you, being dead in your sins and the uncircumsion of your flesh, hath he quickened together with him, having forgiven you all trespasses;
Blotting out the handwriting of ordinances that was against us, which was contrary to us, and took it out of the way, nailing it to his cross;*' (Colossians 2:13, 14)

One of the reasons why we have forgiveness of trespasses is that Jesus blotted out the handwriting of the ordinances of the Old Testament which we have infringed. The record of our trespasses, the punishments resultant thereto, were all taken care of on the cross. They were 'nailed to his cross', and taken out of the way.

Criminal offences have no time limit when it comes to prosecuting a person who commits them. In other words, if a man committed an offence thirty years ago and it became known now, or he is apprehended after hiding all those years, he could still be prosecuted and punished.

A man may have forgotten that he committed certain trespasses, because it may have been so long ago, nevertheless the records are there if he does not repent. Jesus blotted them out, including the records which the enemy keeps to taunt and harass him. You need to deal with this by confession and prayer.

It is important to note that Satan keeps records in the heavenlies and uses them to keep a hold on people and their property, including land.

During deliverance it is important to challenge the enemy and to wipe out those records by reminding the Devil of what Jesus accomplished on the cross and by his blood.

In redeeming land or property which may have been dedicated or devoted to evil spirits by covenants or rituals, the believer needs to forcibly remind Satan, or those spirits, of Christ's work, and have the records of those transactions wiped off Satan's records, by using this scripture.

He Spoiled Principalities and Powers

'And having spoiled principalities and powers, he made a shew of them openly, triumphing over them in it.'
(Colossians 2:15)

It is impossible to imagine the number and size of the

forces of darkness arrayed against us. Even if we knew, it would be impossible to estimate the total weight of their wickedness, their potency and their viciousness, but thanks be to God that Jesus overcame them, spoiled them, made a public show of them and triumphed over them. By this triumph he ensured victory for us in every confrontation we may have with the powers of darkness: if we know how to go about it properly.

Spiritual warfare is a very important aspect of Christian experience, for the very first statement that Jesus made implied it.

> *'And I say also unto thee, That thou art Peter, and upon this rock I will build my church; and the gates of hell shall not prevail against it.'*   (Matthew 16:18)

By this statement, Jesus committed us to spiritual warfare, which would be an instrument of spiritual violence to subdue the gates of hell, meaning the powers of darkness.

At the fall of man, God had made a statement to the serpent:

> *'And I will put enmity between thee and the woman, and between thy seed and her seed; it shall bruise thy head, and thou shalt bruise his heel.'*   (Genesis 3:15)

Jesus had now succeeded in crushing the head of the serpent truly and properly. No wonder he could truly proclaim; *'It is finished.'*

Chapter 14

Revelation of the Glorified Christ

'But on the first day of the week, at early dawn, they came to the tomb, bringing the spices which they had prepared.
And they found the stone rolled away from the tomb, but when they entered, they did not find the body of the Lord Jesus.
And it happened that while they were perplexed about this, behold, two men suddenly stood near them in dazzling apparel; and as the women were terrified and bowed their faces to the ground, the men said to them, "Why do you seek the living One among the dead? He is not here, but He has risen. Remember how He spoke to you while He was still in Galilee, saying that the Son of man must be delivered into the hands of sinful men, and be crucified, and the third day rise again."
And they remembered his words,'

(Luke 24:1–8 NASB)

After seemingly tragic happenings on Calvary, some of the followers went on the first day of the week to the tomb, with spices to embalm Jesus. They were going to embalm a memory, but other things happened. They found the stone rolled away, the tomb empty and angels on guard there. When the angels questioned them as to why they were looking for the 'Living One' among the dead, they remembered his words.

The words that Jesus spoke about his sufferings, crucifixion and resurrection had now come to pass.

A little later in the same chapter, Jesus appeared to two disciples who were walking to Emmaus from Jerusalem and talking about the recent happenings concerning Jesus in Jerusalem. He revealed himself at their destination when they had sat down to eat, and they had to run all the way back to Jerusalem to tell the disciples.

Jesus appeared to selected believers over a period of forty days. He talked with them and in one case told Thomas, the doubter, to put his fingers into his palms and his side.

His remaining disciples now were convinced that Jesus had indeed risen from the dead.

That phase of his early ministry ended, he had to ascend into heaven to sit at God's right hand. When he arrived there, many things took place. First of all God the Father acknowledged that he had done a wonderful job.

> *'But unto the Son he saith, Thy throne, O God, is for ever and ever: a scepter of righteousness is the scepter of thy Kingdom.*
> *Thou hast loved righteousness, and hated iniquity: therefore God, even thy God, hath anointed thee with the oil of gladness above thy fellows,'*

(Hebrews 1:8, 9)

He was also appointed *'heir of all things'* (Hebrews 1:2).

Jesus now wanted the Church to know him in his glorified state. He therefore appeared to John, who was in the Spirit on the Lord's day in the isle of Patmos.

As he began to speak, John turned to see the voice which was speaking to him. The voice introduced itself as The Alpha and Omega. As he turned he saw seven golden candlesticks, and in the midst of the seven candlesticks, Jesus Christ stood clothed with a garment down to his feet, with a golden girdle; his head and hair, white like wool, as white as snow; and his eyes were as a flame of fire.

His feet were like unto fine brass, as if they burned in a furnace, and his voice as the sound of many waters. He held seven stars in his right hand, and out of his mouth went a sharp two-edged sword, while his countenance was as the sun shining in his strength.

> '... *Fear not; I am the first and the last;*
> *I am he that liveth, and was dead;*
> *and, behold, I am alive for evermore,*
> *Amen, and have the keys of hell and of death.'*
>
> (Revelation 1:17, 18)

In this description of himself we now know that we have a Lord and Saviour who lives for evermore; not only that he holds the keys and has authority over the gates of death, and hell, but has triumphed over them.

He then proceeded to dictate letters to the seven churches of Asia, with different introductions of himself in each case. He noted their individual circumstances, their works, and chided or warned or threatened them on their failures. It is interesting to note that he did not write one letter to all the churches, to be read from Jerusalem, but one to each church, with relevant words for each.

He also makes wonderful promises for those who will overcome. This is an inducement for each child of God to strive to overcome.

One incident however, stands out again in this book. It is related in Chapter 5, where God sent an angel to make a proclamation all through heaven and earth for any one who could qualify to step forward to take the book from the hand of him who sits on the throne.

To witness this significant incident, a man was needed to come from the earth, and John was the choice. No man in heaven or earth was found worthy to take the book and to open the seals thereof. There was weeping in heaven when no one was found. I am sure Satan was very far away that day: he could not come near. As for John, an elder who was standing there told him not to weep because the Lion of the Tribe of Judah, the Root of David, had prevailed to open the book and to loose the seven seals thereof.

> *'And I beheld, and lo, in the midst of the throne and of the four beasts, and in the midst of the elders, stood a Lamb as it had been slain, having seven horns and seven eyes, which are the Seven Spirits of God sent forth into all the earth.*
> *And he came and took the book out of the right hand of him that sat upon the throne.'*   (Revelation 5:6–7)

The One who prevailed over sin, curses, the cross, death and hell; the One who overcame principalities and powers and made a public show over them, triumphing over them, stepped forward to collect the book with seven seals. That little book was the title-deed: the certificate of occupancy of the whole world. Jesus who made all things, having died to redeem them, now received the title deed as confirmation of his triumph. In his name therefore, and on the evidence, one can redeem the land from the clutches of the devil, whether it be as a result of covenants, dedications or devotions.

Our Lord prevailed! He is risen from the dead, He is Lord!

When he received the book, there was singing and praise in heaven. The twenty four elders and the four beasts fell down to worship him: they sang a new song. The many angels round about the throne, numbering ten thousand times ten thousand, and thousands of thousands, also sang, and every creature which is in heaven and on earth and in the sea, also blessed the Lord.

> *'Blessing, and honour, and glory, and power, be unto him that sitteth upon the throne, and unto the Lamb for ever and ever. And the four beasts said, Amen.*

And the four and twenty elders fell down and worshipped him that liveth for ever and ever.'

(Revelation 5:13–14)

Chapter 15

The Names of Jesus

In 1 Timothy 6:15, He is called *'the blessed and only Potentate, the King of Kings and the Lord of Lords.'*

In John 14:6, He is called, *'the Way, the Truth and the Life.'*

In Hebrews 12:2, He is called *'the Author and finisher of our faith.'*

In Song of Solomon 2:1, He is called, *'the Lily of the valley.'*

In Isaiah 9:6, He is called, *'Wonderful, Counsellor, The mighty God The everlasting Father, The Prince of Peace.'*

In Revelation 5:5, He is called, *'the Lion of the tribe of Judah, the root of David.'*

In John 9:5, He is called, *'the Light of the world.'*

In John 6:36, He is called, *'the Bread of Life.'*

In John 4:25, 26, He is called, *'the Messiah.'*

In Matthew 16:16, He is called, *'Christ, the Son of the Living God.'*

In Daniel 7:9, He is called, *'the Ancient of Days.'*

In Revelation 1:8, He is called, *'the Alpha and the Omega.'*

In Revelation 2:8, He is called, *'the First and the Last.'*

In Revelation 2:12, He is called, *'he which hath the sharp sword with two edges.'*

In Revelation 3:1, He is called, *'he that hath the seven Spirits of God.'*

In Revelation 5:10, He is called, *'the Lamb.'*

In Revelation 19:11, He is called, *'Faithful and True.'*
In Revelation 19:13, He is called, *'the Word of God.'*
In Revelation 22:13, He is called, *'Alpha and Omega, the beginning and the end, the first and the last.'*
In Revelation 22:16, He is called, *'the root of the off-spring of David and the bright and morning star.'*

Get to know Jesus Christ by repenting of your sins, confessing them, asking Him for forgiveness, and inviting him into your heart as your personal Saviour. Give him your spirit, your soul and your body: for they are rightly his.

If you have already known him, rededicate your life to him and serve him more fervently, for he saith, Surely I come quickly.

> *'And behold I come quickly; and my reward is with me, to give every man according as his work shall be. I am Alpha and Omega, the beginning and the end, the first and the last.'* (Revelation 22:12–13)

The grace of our Lord Jesus Christ be with you all. Amen.

Contact Address

The Author

Emeka Nwankpa
48 Faulks Road
PO Box 4930
ABA
Nigeria